Ibsen's Dramatic Technique

The Smiling Ibsen, by Erik Werenskiold

Ibsen's
Dramatic Technique

by

P. F. D. TENNANT

Sometime Fellow of Queens' College
in the University of Cambridge

HUMANITIES PRESS
New York
1 9 6 5

First Published 1948

Reprinted 1965 by
Humanities Press Inc.
by special arrangement with
Bowes & Bowes Ltd.

Library of Congress Catalog Card Number: 65-28122

Printed in U.S.A. by
NOBLE OFFSET PRINTERS, INC.
NEW YORK 3, N. Y.

CONTENTS

ILLUSTRATIONS

PREFACE

It is with some diffidence that I add this book to the already voluminous literature on Ibsen. I only do so in the hope that it may make some contribution to the understanding of a great dramatist whose own works, unlike the great majority of books written about him, will always remain a monument of literature. The theme of this study is justified in so far as it has not been examined at length before. To those who have little or no knowledge of Ibsen I hope it may give an appetite to learn more. To those who are well acquainted with the man and his works I trust it may offer another method of approach for further appreciation.

I ask the indulgence of my readers for any inaccuracies which they may find in the text. These, I fear, are inevitable in a work which was written before the war and which I have now revised without access to much essential material only available in Scandinavia or among my own manuscripts in Cambridge.

This is not an omnibus work on Ibsen. It is not concerned with his life, his philosophy or his conception of human nature. These subjects are only touched upon in so far as they concern his stage technique. For purposes of reference, however, I have included a chronology of Ibsen's life and works to which the reader can turn for dates and biographical details. I would in fact advise those not already acquainted with the details of Ibsen's life to skim through this chronology before beginning the book. I have also added a select bibliography for those who care to pursue the study of Ibsen. I would stress that this is a 'select' bibliography, and a purely subjective selection at that, out of the thousands of good, bad and indifferent works devoted to the great poet and dramatist.

I owe a deep debt of gratitude to many friends in Cambridge and in the Scandinavian countries for their help and encouragement in my pursuit of Scandinavian studies in the past fifteen years. It is to them that I offer this book as a token of thanks and an earnest of my continued interest in these studies in our country. First and foremost I must mention the late Professor Anna Paues, to whose kindness and patient encouragement I, like so many others, owe my love of things Scandinavian. Secondly I owe an expression of thanks to the Cambridge Scandinavian Fund for

enabling me to pursue the research out of which this book origi-
nated. Last but not least, my thanks are due to friends and pupils
in the University and to members of the Cambridge Scandinavian
Society whose interest contributed to a wider understanding of
Scandinavian life and literature in our country before the war.

I wish to acknowledge with thanks the kind permission of the
editors of *The Modern Language Review* in allowing me to reprint
a previous contribution to that journal. My thanks are also due
to Professor Francis Bull for similar permission to reprint a contribution to *Edda*. Further I am most grateful to the librarians of
the Oslo University Library, of the Bergen Museum, and the
Manager of the Royal Theatre, Copenhagen, for giving me access
to their manuscript collections and permitting me to reproduce as
illustrations certain significant documents in facsimile.

P. F. D. TENNANT

British Embassy
Paris

April 1946

To
PROFESSOR FRANCIS BULL
of Oslo University

Ibsen's Dramatic Technique

INTRODUCTION

ON January 9th, 1887, Ibsen attended the epoch-making production of *Ghosts* at Anno's Residenztheater in Berlin, and the realism of the performance was such that it resulted in the omission of the following well-known lines of Mrs. Alving's: 'It was then that I began to examine the seams of your teaching. I wanted only to undo a single stitch; but when I had loosened it, the whole lot came undone. And then I understood that it was all machine sewn.' Ibsen asked the producer why he had omitted the words and received the reply: 'Modern sewing machines have been so perfected that it is impossible to undo the stitches.' Ibsen answered, smiling: 'You can rest assured that Mrs. Alving up at Rosenvold has still got her old-fashioned sewing machine.'

It was with this highly romantic and unrealistic play, with its Greek atmosphere of destiny brooding over the haunting family tragedy, that Ibsen established his international fame as a modern realistic dramatist. Julius Hoffory ran up and down the auditorium between the acts exclaiming: 'To-day a new era has dawned for German literature.' It was the first of Ibsen's plays to be produced by Antoine in Paris in 1890 and was the most popular item on his repertoire during his tours of France and Italy. It was the first play of Ibsen's to shock the English public when it was performed by J. T. Grein's Independent Theatre at the Royalty in London on March 13th, 1891. The abusive criticism of the British press of the day has become classical. The *Pall Mall Gazette* called it 'an open drain', 'naked loathsomeness', 'a putrid play', and Ibsen was immortalized when the critic concluded his diatribe with the words, 'Old Ibsen is as dead as a door-nail'. It has remained a box-office draw for the realistic theatre ever since.

Ghosts has been acclaimed as a realistic play, and much of Ibsen's drama has been labelled realistic accordingly. But nothing could be more misleading. Gordon Craig was the first to insist on this when he wrote, 'Ibsen's detestation of realism is nowhere more apparent than in his two plays *Rosmersholm* and *Ghosts*'. He designed his spacious setting for the play in conscious opposition to the typical realistic *décor* which tried to produce the illusion of the 'fourth wall' by using the footlights as a fireplace and arranging the room accordingly, quite regardless of the fact that it is unusual in everyday life to conceal oneself in a chimney when observing the doings of other people. Ibsen, when writing the play, talked of realism; but when realism was exaggerated to such an extent as in the Berlin performance he himself was the first to ridicule it. It is forgotten by many that theatrical art is based essentially on conventions, that these conventions are dictated largely by the nature of the audience, and that it is upon the acceptance of these conventions that dramatic illusion depends. It is equally conventional and unrealistic to imagine oneself to be sitting in a chimney as to accept a seventeenth-century actor in clocked stockings, buckled shoes and knee breeches and a tinselled wig as a convincing representation of an Oriental potentate.

Dramatic illusion depends on the identification of the audience with what is on the stage. This identification is impossible unless the spectators, in buying their tickets, surrender their right to numerous everyday conceptions before entering the fictional world of the theatre, indulging, as Coleridge says, in 'willing suspension of disbelief'. What we know as dramatic realism is in fact only a series of conventions; but the existence of these conventions has been obscured by the approximation of setting, costume, character and diction to the conventions of the world outside the theatre. Thus the spectator is no longer conscious of that sense of relief and excitement on entering the theatre, he no longer discards his identity in the cloakroom, but brings the same mental faculties to bear on his judgment of the play as those with which he forms his opinions in everyday life.

Ibsen's realism, which gave the great impulse to the realistic drama of modern times, always remained only an approximation to contemporary life, and never descended to the unpoetic drabness of the naturalistic school and that of his own numerous imitators. We need only turn to one of Ibsen's most 'realistic' plays, *Ghosts*, to see how conventional and unrealistic the play actually is, though it created an illusion of everyday life for Ibsen's contemporaries. This he did by the use of contemporary characters, contemporary dialogue, a contemporary indoor setting and an adherence to the conventions of the unities. How unrealistic and romantic is the fate *motif* which dominates the play. Coincidences are skilfully given the appearance of consequences. The sins of the fathers are visited on the children in the most irrational manner.

14

Regine, who is Osvald's sister, has opportunely escaped inheriting the venereal disease from which Osvald suffers. The incestuous love of brother and sister is a time-honoured ingredient of romantic fate—tragedy, and the rest of the devices are equally traditional. In the same room, in the same circumstances as her mother with Osvald's father, Regine reproves Osvald for his advances with identically the same words. Nothing could finally be more unrealistic than Osvald's sudden physical decomposition in the last act, a feature which was defended tooth and nail by Ibsen's contemporaries against the sceptical disquisitions of doctors in Germany and Scandinavia, who seriously considered it worth while to disprove the possibility of such an occurrence in real life, and thereby hoped they had diminished the value of the play as a work of art.

Ibsen was furious at these interpretations, and his anger knew no bounds when his previous play, *A Doll's House*, was appreciated not as a drama but as a *cause célèbre*, putting him into the false position of an agitator for women's rights, while lawyers seriously discussed the pros and cons of Nora's legal position. The acceptance of Ibsen's plays as reality and not as drama has enriched theatrical history with innumerable incidents which far surpass such apocryphal stories as that of the indignant American officer who shot Iago from the auditorium, of the old lady who warned Polonius behind the arras, or of the farmer who offered Richard III a horse for a far lower price than he was prepared to pay. Ibsen's contemporaries, and many of his critics and commentators, failed to observe the ritual of handing over their identity with their coats in the cloakroom as they came to the theatre, and walked in, bringing with them the conventions and prejudices of ordinary life, not adopting those of the stage.

The failure of Ibsen's contemporaries to distinguish between fact and fiction was due to Ibsen's skill in letting his plays centre round the burning moral or social problems of the day. This at least is true as far as his earlier modern plays are concerned. But nowadays the perspective of time makes it easier to consider Ibsen as a dramatist and artist and not as a moralist. His ideas have not stood the test of time as well as the characters which enunciate them, but the dramatic effect of his technique is as fresh as ever. He was not an original thinker, but he had the faculty for presenting second-hand ideas as human problems, in a

15

dramatic form which gives his conflicts an illusion of depth and appears to endue his characters with flesh and blood. It is Ibsen's dramatic form, and not his ideas, which constitutes his great contribution to the theatre. From his earliest days he insisted on illusion and not reality as the basis of art, and in the following chapters we shall be able to trace the evolution of the technique with which Ibsen achieved his illusion and to investigate the conventions which became the ingredients of his realism.

CHAPTER I

IBSEN'S METHOD OF COMPOSITION
AND
THE NATURE OF HIS INSPIRATION

MANY of Ibsen's friends and acquaintances have given us impressions of the dramatist at work. Henrik Jaeger, who visited him at Sæby in 1887 to collect material for his subsequent biography, gives perhaps the best account. He writes as follows:

'When he has chosen a subject, he thinks it over long and carefully, without putting pen to paper. Much of this thinking work is carried out on his walks; also the long time he takes dressing is made use of for these preliminary ponderings.

'When the whole has been thought over in broad outline he writes a plan. I asked him: ''I suppose you work out your plan so carefully that you for that matter could easily write the last act first and the first act last?'' ''No'', he answered. ''Many of the details only occur to me during the process of composition, bit by bit as I get along.''

'On the basis of the plan he sets to work on the shaping of the play, which is a relatively swift undertaking. He is always careful when finishing work one day to have quite an amount of dialogue complete in his mind, with which he can begin the next morning; by this means he thinks he gets started better. If however he happens to get stuck, he does not give up for that day but continues to think and work until he has got going with his work again.

'By this means the first draft develops from day to day until it is finished.

'But this manuscript is for Ibsen no more than a piece of preliminary work. Only when he has completed this does he think he is becoming intimate with his characters, so that he knows their habits and their manner of expression completely.

'Then comes the work of revision in the second version and finally the fair copy in the third; he does not dispatch his work until the fair copy is fully completed. He preserves the earlier manuscripts. ''One day I shall present them to my son, so he can

17

do what he likes with them.'' He regrets having once handed over the manuscript of *Brand* to a Danish collector. ''I don't like people seeing what stupidities I was guilty of before I got my work into the shape I wanted'', he said.'

Jaeger then tells how Ibsen worked with great regularity for not more than four hours a day, from nine in the morning until one o'clock, on a ration of one roll and a cup of strong coffee. After lunch he would rest and for the remainder of the day go out walking, visiting cafés and fulfilling his social duties.

There is, however, a curious dualism between the outward figure of Ibsen as it was known to his contemporaries and the inward man who conceived the great artistic monument which we possess to-day. The outward man was reserved and correct in the extreme. He felt the power of social disapproval in his early youth when his father's bankruptcy had brought disgrace upon the family, and his outward life from this time on became a frenzied effort to enlist the respect of those about him. We know he developed very regular habits as he grew older. The social equilibrium for which he was striving he succeeded in attaining round about 1869 at the age of forty-one. It expressed itself in the most ridiculous self-complacency. He had now become a figure of importance and for the first time in his life he had met real success with *Brand* and *Peer Gynt*. In this year he wrote to his friend Lorentz Dietrichson giving instructions for the biographical note which was to be prefixed to the first German translation of *Brand*, with the words: 'A poet's hardships are no longer a draw; describe preferably how the government and parliament have granted me a stipend, how I travel, am living in dem grossen Vaterlande, etc.' Financial security makes of him a pedantic business man and it is from now on that Hegel of Gyldendal, in Copenhagen, becomes his publisher and Ibsen begins to watch with an eagle eye over his interests. He speculates on the best dates for publication and finally decides for the Christmas market, he buys Government securities with his royalties, invests shrewdly in new companies recommended by Hegel and makes a fortune in Oslo tramway shares.

There are various other signs of his self-assurance at this time. He altered his handwriting and changed from his earlier forward-slanting, fluent, pointed hand to a pedantic, rounded, backward-slanting calligraphy. The first instance of this is in the fair copy of *The League of Youth*. In his letter to Dietrichson he enclosed a

18

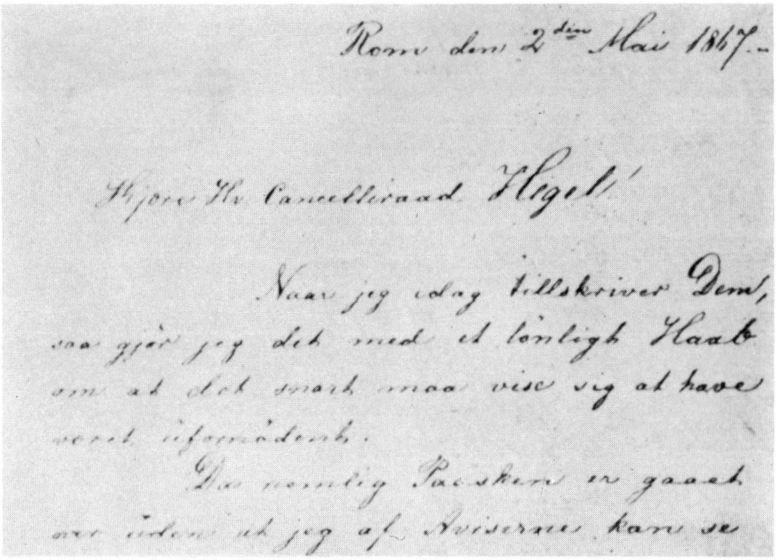
Rom den 2den Mai 1867.

Kjære Hr Cancelliraad Hegel!

Naar jeg idag tillskriver Dem, saa gjør jeg det med et lönligt Haab om at det snart maa vise sig at have været uformödent.

Da nemlig Paasken er gaaet over uden at jeg af Aviserne kan se

1867

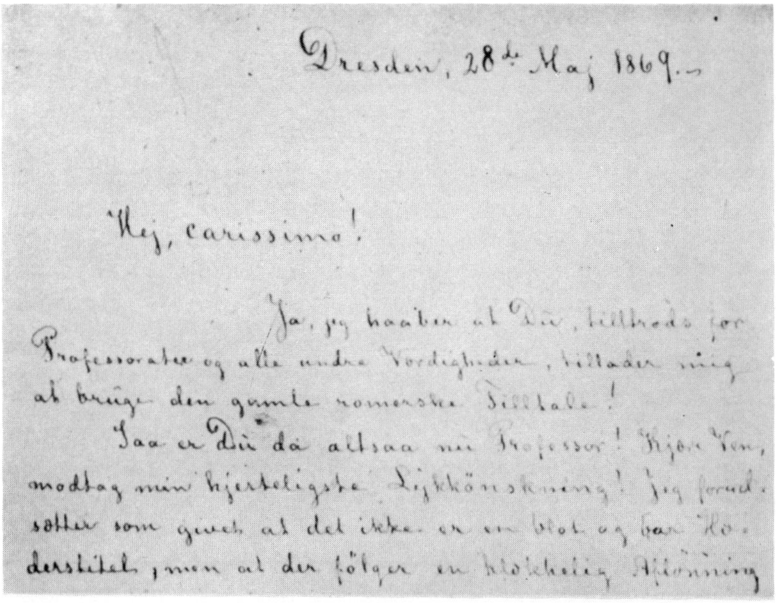
Dresden, 28de Maj 1869.

Hej, carissimo!

Ja, jeg haaber at Du, tilltrods for Professoratet og alle andre Værdigheder, tillader mig at bruge den gamle romerske Tilltale!

Saa er Du da altsaa nu Professor! Kjære Ven, modtag min hjerteligste Lykönskning! Jeg forudsætter som givet at det ikke er en blot og bar Hæderstitel, men at der fölger en klækkelig Afløning

1869

Specimens of Ibsen's Handwriting

photograph of himself. He had shaved off his beard, was wearing fashionable dundreary whiskers and was dressed in a smart velvet smoking jacket. When in the same year he visited Stockholm, people were surprised to find that the author of the ascetic *Brand* was in fact a dapper man of the world. He now began to value highly the approbation of society, and started his childish collection of decorations, which he wore at the slightest provocation. He was given his first this very year, and his second not long after when he was sent as a deputy to the opening of the Suez Canal. The rest of his life he spent collecting them. He received from now on one recognition after another. A grant was given him by the Society of Sciences in Trondheim, and another was voted him by the Government for the study of Swedish culture. It is significant that from now dates his final break with Norway, which he had left before finishing *Brand*. He never returned there to live until 1891, when repeated requests sufficiently flattered his vanity. A personal liberation of importance was a final rupture with the painful associations of his youth, when he paid his last contribution to the upkeep of an illegitimate child he had had with a servant girl when working as an apothecary's apprentice in Grimstad fourteen years earlier, a nagging reminder of his past, which he threw off his chest in the figure of the green woman and her child in *Peer Gynt*. From now on he begins to preserve his manuscripts. It is remarkable how all the earlier drafts and manuscript notes are missing, whereas from this date onwards Ibsen began to document himself as a person of consequence, and never failed to preserve and date the most insignificant jottings. Many of his earlier manuscripts were, however, auctioned or destroyed by his creditors after he left Norway. He began to feel so indispensable to the world at large that he started to take the most meticulous care of himself. He never went for long walks or climbed hills for fear of straining his heart; he slept long, did not work too long, avoided stimulants while working, wrapped himself up in his frock-coat for fear of colds, and wore the inevitable top-hat to preserve his dignity and protect him from any chance tile that might fall on his head and end his days before the fulfilment of his mission. His habits became as regular as clockwork. From his later years in Munich, from 1880 onwards, he systematized his daily programme. He would work for three hours in the morning, eating a breakfast of rolls and black coffee. From 12 to 1 he sat in the Hotel Achatz drinking his morning pint. In the afternoon he would go for a walk, observing the habits of men and dogs. He soon became one of the sights of the town. He took to frequenting the Zum Hoftheater restaurant, but when the proprietor put a stove in the place of his regular seat, he moved in protest to the Café Maximilian. Here he could be seen every day between 6.30 and 7.30 sitting at the second or third round table to the left of the entrance with a glass of dark beer or a brandy and a carafe of water in front of him. Here he would read the newspapers from cover to cover. For the benefit of onlookers he would pose in the attitude of an absorbed genius, his left hand on his thigh and his right hand poised as if in the act of writing. At 7.30 he took his umbrella and top-hat and black gloves, and shuffled out slowly. He would often work at home in his shirt-sleeves, but preserved decencies out of doors by always adopting an air of distant detachment and walking in his frock-coat and top-hat ten paces ahead of his wife when they were out on airings together. His life at home after 1891 was equally regular. He would take a walk in the morning, and at midday would proceed down Carl Johan to his seat at the Grand Hotel, where there was a chair reserved for Dr. Henrik Ibsen. During the latter years of his life he became more and more unapproachable and shut up in himself away from reality.

This regularity was extended from hours to years, and from 1877 to 1899 his work was subject to a regular manic-depressive periodicity of production, writing one play every two years with clockwork punctuality for the Christmas book market. The only two exceptions are *The Enemy of the People*, which was written in one year, and his last play, *When We Dead Awaken*, which appeared after an interval of three years. His most active period of work extended from early summer to autumn.

This was the outward figure Ibsen presented to the world. One can hardly say that, regarded from the point of view of experience, Ibsen's work can be conceived as a reflection of this outward man. But as we have seen, his outward man was a studied pose, a fortification behind which to conceal himself. The real man is revealed in the fixed pattern of themes which recur in his work. He kept painful reality at a distance by projecting it into his work, or realized in his art, desires which moral cowardice forbade him to fulfil in his life. The conflict of art and life is a fundamental theme of Ibsen's work, from his earliest poems onwards, and recurs again and again in the figures of poets and artists who fail hopelessly to come to grips with circumstances. That this conflict was felt by Ibsen himself there is no doubt whatsoever.

The dramatist more than all other artists finds in his work an escape from responsibility or a means of procuring social recognition. He often attains both of these objects at once. He, like the actor, can taste the inestimable pleasure of yielding to his lower instincts, identifying himself with a despicable criminal and receiving applause for the satisfaction of his desires without exposing himself to any social inconvenience. With his higher instincts it is the same. He can escape from reality into the realms of imagination and find a similar consolation. Many forms of art exist which do not exhibit themselves and do not require an audience. It is inconceivable, however, to think of a play being written except in terms of author, actor, audience. The ones that are not written with this end in view are bad plays.

Now Ibsen was a dramatist to the finger tips. Even the majority of his poems he wrote with the conscious desire of producing a dramatic effect. His first poems were written as a young man in Grimstad in the form of epigrams about local personalities, and they were circulated anonymously, so that the author might have the pleasure of witnessing their results without fear of consequences. In his dramas we see the same desire to project inconvenient feelings and to cause a sensation for which he could not be held morally responsible.

Ibsen's dramatic tendencies were born of a spirit of revenge. His childhood was decidedly depressing, in spite of his suspiciously exaggerated description of its hardships. His youth was an uphill struggle of the worst kind, and he was constantly disappointed till the age of 38, when he met with his first great success. This resulted in the change of mood of which I have spoken above, his feeling of self-assurance, and his adoption of a fictitious personality. From now on his life becomes a reckoning with the past. Not until he has revenged himself on Norway does he venture to return there for good at the age of 63, not until he has completely settled with his past does he lay down his pen to die. The older he gets the further back his memory probes, and the theme-pattern of his work is completed by the perfection of this jigsaw puzzle of recollections of early defeats and disasters.

Like many great artists, Ibsen had a supreme contempt for his kind. With Thomas Mann, he sees in art a substitute for life, and the large majority of his plays introduce the conflict of art and life. But whereas his youthful romanticism always gave the prize to the artist or idealist who was loyal to his calling in spite of the temptations held out by life, his conscience later began to plague him when he realized the tragedy of his own incurable aestheticism. He saw himself as the great artist who had risen to the heights of fame only at the expense of his own life and the lives of others, and in his later plays we find him holding out life as the greater good. The artist-characters in his plays are condensations of personal experience. The poet Jatgeir in *The Pretenders*, like Ibsen himself, found a compensation for life in his grief-inspired poetry; Osvald the painter is a doomed man; Hjalmar Ekdal has found a refuge from life by posing as an artist and believing in the inspiration which never comes; Lyngstrand is consumptive and paints garish pictures; Solness deadens his evil conscience by building houses; and Professor Rubek in Ibsen's last play exploits the affections and the body of his model to create an immortal work of sculpture. The principles underlying the creative process of Ibsen's artist-characters are illuminating in that they give a clue to Ibsen's own form of artistic creation. In Hjalmar Ekdal he drew a brilliant satire of the romantic artist with his long hair, ample necktie and eccentric clothes, who takes a nap after lunch every day and hopes to wake up with the inspiration that is never forthcoming. Ibsen, however, far from dissociating himself from this artist figure, felt the strongest sympathy with him, and it is an example of the strictest artistic honesty that he could so identify himself with the character.

He was himself the victim of inspiration, and with him it was of an almost physical nature. It took the most primitive forms of compensation for emotional frustration. When he was jilted by his first love he found consolation in an elegiac mood with his first poem 'Resignation'. Anger and revenge were again another form his inspiration took. When he was thrown over by Rikke Holst in Bergen he wrote *Lady Inger of Ostrât*, which he describes as being based on 'a love affair, begun in haste and ending with a violent rupture'. His marriage gave him greater self-assurance, and in *Love's Comedy* he castigates the conventions of middle-class society which had so long held him down. *Brand* was a work of revenge against the moral hypocrisy and lukewarmness of his countrymen. The shape of the play came to him as a sudden revelation while visiting St. Peter's at Rome, and he describes in a letter to P. Hansen how his anger took the form of poetry. 'While I was writing *Brand* I had a scorpion in an empty beer glass standing on my table. From time to time the creature became ill; then I would throw it a piece of luscious fruit which it attacked wildly and injected with its poison; then it became well again. Isn't it much the same with us poets? The laws of nature apply also in the spheres of art.'

Such direct acknowledgment of inspiration as a euphemistic name for the more elementary emotions is typical of Ibsen's aesthetic fatalism and intellectual honesty. His creative processes are governed subconsciously by a certain fixed pattern of obsessions which are apparent in the themes and situations of his work.

The basic situation in all his work is the family complex. His scope is nearly always restricted to family and private relations; only in *Peer Gynt* and *Emperor and Galilean* can it be said that the issues at stake overstep the bounds of this narrow circle. This restriction accounts for the recurring themes of family problems, of marriage, of the relations between parents and children, of heredity, of individual emancipation, of incest and of illegitimacy. These problems are only given a moral significance in the earlier plays, but as Ibsen himself becomes more emancipated from his past, pathological and sexual factors are introduced into his method of psychological motivation. With Hedda Gabler and Rebekka West, for instance, we are far removed from figures like Furia and Aurelia in Ibsen's first play *Catilina*, which are merely personifications of the forces of good and evil. Ibsen's memory becomes more lively as he gets older and gains assurance for his revenge.

The situation in Ibsen's own family seems to form a background upon the pattern of which the situations of his plays are constructed. His relation to his parents was strange. He left home just before his sixteenth birthday, and it is said that he only returned home once before moving to Oslo as a student in 1850. He returned to his family town Skien twice later, in 1859 and 1860, but only to beg for money from his uncle, and without seeing his parents. His explanations for this estrangement are specious. Once he excused himself on the grounds of the pietist element in his home, which in fact hardly existed. Later he said that pride forbade him to return till he had sufficient money to show his face as an independent person, in spite of the fact that he had never been financially dependent on his parents. But an attitude of emotional dependence on them pursued him till a late period in his life. When his mother died in 1869 he waited several months before answering his sister's letter announcing her death. When his old rake of a father Knud Ibsen died in 1877 he wrote to his uncle and thanked him for the care he had taken of the drink-sodden old degenerate, but expressed no grief at his death, and personal accounts tell how unperturbed he was when he received the news. Ibsen has himself said that he used his father and mother as the models for various characters in his plays. His mother is the prototype of the self-effacing woman who appears again and again in Ibsen's work, first with Inga in the *Pretenders* and Aase in *Peer Gynt*, while the type occurs for the last time with Ella Rentheim in *John Gabriel Borkman*. The father is alluded to as the old ragamuffin Jon Gynt, but is treated for the first time with full objectivity and humour in the figure of Old Ekdal in *The Wild Duck* in 1884, when Ibsen was fifty-six. Osvald's outburst against filial piety in *Ghosts* three years before is an instance of the way in which the family situation still rankled in Ibsen's memory. It is astounding that his childhood should exercise such a strong influence over him as a grown man, but his life is a remarkable instance of a man's incapacity to grow up owing to early emotional reverses which are not overcome in later life.

If we examine Ibsen's childhood we can understand how it had the power to control his artistic production in later life. He was the eldest of the family, two years older than his brother Johan Andreas. From the start he was left on his own to find his way without the help of elder sisters and brothers. With a self-effacing mother and a boisterous scoundrel of a father he was torn between loyalties to both and was left to solve the situation by himself. There are also mysteries about Ibsen's birth which probably without reason made him have doubts about his origin. He was born on March 20th, 1828, in Skien. The statements of Ibsen's own father and traditions in the town support the belief that he was born in the house of a family friend Wamberg, while Ibsen himself always sedulously took care to state that he was born in the family house of Stockmannsgården. His father seemed to like to spread an air of mystery about the birthplace of his son, and this probably fostered a suspicion and a wish in Ibsen himself that he might after all not be his father's son, a phenomenon very well known to psychologists. Anyhow, such suspicions would have only given additional strength to an aversion which Ibsen had felt for his father at an early age. An affection for his mother, which was perhaps rather pity than anything else, helped to group his parents in his mind in a relationship which pursued him all through life and stultified his emotional development. His father's bankruptcy, and the family's social ignominy when he was no more than eight years old, fixed the situation indelibly in his mind.

His emotional life offers many examples of what we would expect from such an upbringing. He became shy and retiring, and took little part in what other children were doing around him. His only love affairs were irresponsible ones. He had his first at Grimstad with a servant girl ten years older than himself who gave birth to a child. He had two subsequent love affairs on an ethereal plane with girls of good family, Clara Ebbel and Rikke Holst. In both of these his suit was rejected and he was made to appear ridiculous. Finally he took the course of irresponsibility and married Susannah Thoresen for whom he need enter into no competition and whom he could satisfactorily identify with the image of his mother. She was lame and unkempt, and the first time they met they wallflowered together at a dance. According to all accounts she was a depressing personality, and Ibsen began to realize this when in his old age he tried to recapture the life he had lost and to have small flirtations with successions of young girls, experiences which again never demanded any responsible acts of choice on his part.

Out of the family situation, in which Ibsen himself had been involved and which had been so disastrous for his happiness in after life, developed the fixed pattern of family relationships we see in his plays, a pattern which is repeated and repeated again and again until it no longer represents a danger to him. His characters in the plays up to *A Doll's House* quite often succeed in freeing themselves from these situations and fulfilling Ibsen's own wish which he was unable to carry out in practice. The father-mother-son and mother-father-daughter triangle recurs in his work with unfailing regularity. We only have to think of Lady Inger and her son, of Gregers Werle and the memory of his mother, of Mrs.

Alving and Osvald, of Aase and Peer Gynt, of Mrs. Borkman and Erhard and of Hedda Gabler and the memory of her father. Of the latter Ibsen wrote to his French translator Count Prozor that he called the play *Hedda Gabler* because he considered the heroine as the daughter of her father and not as the wife of Tesman. The theme of illegitimacy occurs often, a subject which may have obessed Ibsen himself. It plays a part in *Lady Inger*, in *Ghosts*, in *The Wild Duck*, in *Rosmersholm* and in *Little Eyolf*. Incest also is a salient feature of *Ghosts*, *Rosmersholm* and *Little Eyolf*.

· It is this pathological element which inspires the themes and situations and characters of many of Ibsen's plays. In his early work it is mostly suppressed and given the form of ideas, but in the later plays ideas and reality go side by side, and gradually the ideas begin to recede into the background. In his young days he had hoped to free himself of his obsessions by talking of man's vocation, the true marriage, truth and freedom and the realization of the individual, but with *The Wild Duck* and *Rosmersholm* these ideas are subordinated to the fate of the individuals themselves, which is directed by irrational impulses over which the mind no longer has control. It is now that the family situation is portrayed as belonging no more to the realms of philosophy and ideas but to those of pure human relationships. It is now that Ibsen for the first time can portray the family situation without symbolical circumlocution, and it is significant that with the portrait of Old Ekdal in *The Wild Duck* he frees himself for the first time of his emotional attitude of protest to his father and characterizes him with humorous objectivity. Variations on the family theme compose the majority of the plots of Ibsen's plays, and it seems as though Ibsen's whole career as a dramatist was conditioned by a desire to get even with a state of affairs which had made his childhood and youth such painful memories for him.

Having now considered the nature of Ibsen's inspiration, let us turn to the factors which shaped it into dramatic form. Firstly there is Ibsen's outstanding quality of vision. He himself said that 'to be a poet is to see'. He was no mean painter and he certainly had the faculty of visualizing all he wrote. When writing he was sometimes under the influence of hallucinations, and was unable to distinguish between reality and the creatures of his imagination. While working on *A Doll's House* he was nervous and retiring and lived in a world alone, which gradually became peopled with his own imaginary characters. Once he suddenly remarked to his wife: 'Now I have seen Nora. She came right up to me and put her hand on my shoulder.' 'How was she dressed?' asked his wife. 'She had a simple blue cotton dress,' he replied without hesitation. Besides visualizing them he also grew intimate with his characters while creating them, and when he sent his manuscript of *The Wild Duck* to Hegel he wrote: '. . . I am sending you the MS. of my new play, *The Wild Duck*, which has occupied me daily for the last four months, and from which I now cannot part without a certain feeling of regret. The people in this play, in spite of their numerous weaknesses, have none the less after continuous daily intercourse become dear to me . . . .' So intimate had Ibsen become with Nora while at work on *A Doll's House* that when John Paulsen asked him why she was called Nora, Ibsen replied in a matter-of-fact tone: 'She was really called Leonora, you know, but everyone called her Nora, since she was the spoilt child of the family.' This intimacy was of course often due to the fact that Ibsen was using people he knew as models for his characters. Laura Kieler, whose domestic troubles he exploited for *A Doll's House*, continually reproached him for his breach of confidence, and it is significant that the dress she wore on the occasion of her last visit to Ibsen just before he wrote *When We Dead Awaken* is described exactly in the black and white robe which Irene wears in the play. These faculties of vision and intimacy concern not only the characters but also their surroundings, and will be discussed separately with reference to the staging of Ibsen's plays.

Ibsen was also extremely sensitive to his surroundings when writing, and much of the atmosphere of his plays is influenced by the circumstances under which they were written. 'Surroundings', he wrote, 'have a great influence on the forms in which imagination creates. Can I not, almost like Christoff in Jakob v. Tyboe, point out Brand and Peer Gynt and say: "Look, that was a bout of wine-drinking"? And is there not in *The League of Youth* something which reminds one of Knackwurst and Bier?' (*Brand* and *Peer Gynt* were written in Italy and the latter play in Dresden.) After writing the dull ideological pseudo-German world-historic drama *Emperor and Galilean*, Ibsen moved from protestant Dresden to catholic Munich and wrote to his friend Daae: 'By moving to Munich I shall unfortunately be further away from home, but on the other hand I shall be a good deal nearer Italy and shall at the same time have the pleasure of living among catholics, who are without question preferable to protestants here in Germany.' On another occasion he described the influence of surroundings on his development and traced his evolution from being a Norwegian to a Scandinavian and finally a Germanic poet. His work is permeated with the atmosphere of his surroundings, and, like all Scandinavian poets, one theme is to be traced in nearly all his work, the contrast of north and south, the longing of the northerner to escape from snow and ice and to come to sunshine, vegetation and warmth. Much of the drabness of a wet summer in Gossensass, where Ibsen wrote *Ghosts*, helps to give an illusion of the drizzly west coast of Norway to the play, while the thrill of his first real acquaintance with the sea at Molde in Norway and Sæby in Denmark is transferred to the seaside holiday atmosphere of *The Lady from the Sea*.

Two other factors controlling his inspiration are a desire for concentration and elimination. These can be studied in the development of the final play from the original plans and intermediate versions. *Pillars of Society* was for instance early conceived in five acts and these were reduced to four, while the scene which originally changed in each act is finally restricted to one and the same room for all. In *A Doll's House* the earlier versions contain discourses on Darwinism which are later eliminated as superfluous and are transformed into action. In the same way the second act of the earlier versions of *The Wild Duck* is full of hunting reminiscences exchanged between Gregers and Old Ekdal, while these are omitted in the final play and are replaced by Ekdal's active hunting in the attic with live rabbits as his game. In the earliest jottings of plans for *Hedda Gabler* we see that the second act was originally to have taken place in the garden. Remains of this are to be seen in the draft version of Act II which Ibsen only just began and then crossed out, to transfer the scene to the interior of the house where the whole of the play is enacted. In the interest of dramatic concentration Ibsen often entirely eliminates characters who have figured in earlier versions of plays, and when he is convinced of their dramatic potentialities he frequently makes use of them in subsequent work. In *Pillars of Society*, for instance, Ibsen originally included Bernick's mother, a tutor Evensen and old Mads Tönnesen. These are all later eliminated and Mads Tönnesen turns up again as 'the badger', Morten Kiil, one of the central figures of *An Enemy of the People*. In *Rosmersholm* Rosmer originally had two daughters whom Ibsen finally dispensed with and used instead as Hilde and Bolette in *The Lady from the Sea*, while Hilde puts in an appearance again in *The Master Builder*. In the plans of *The Lady from the Sea* we meet 'the old married clerk. Has in his youth written a play, which has been produced once. Files and polishes it endlessly and lives under the illusion of having it published and making his name'. He is cut out and appears again as a finished character, the clerk Foldal, in *John Gabriel Borkman*. In Ibsen's last play, *When We Dead Awaken*, he had originally allowed for numerous superfluous characters, who were subsequently eradicated, finally shrinking the number of actual protagonists to four.

Another tendency can be traced in the development of Ibsen's manuscripts, the gradual individualization of his characters. While occupied with the writing of *The Wild Duck*, Ibsen wrote to Brandes that he was concentrating on 'perfecting the finesses of the dialogue and the more energetic individualization of character and diction'. We see how the various versions show Ibsen's method of individualizing certain characters and portions of the setting in the play at the expense of others which form a background. While the earlier versions show characters not later included, the three chamberlains who are guests at Werle's dinner party are described as follows: 'Chamberlain Flor (the one with the anecdotes), Chamberlain Rasmussen (satirist), Chamberlain Sæther (gallant, stupid).' In the first draft they retain their names, likewise in the second, though Rasmussen is changed to Kaspersen. But in the play they appear as a 'flabby-faced gentleman', a 'short-sighted gentleman', and a 'thin-haired gentleman'. In contrast to them the other characters are correspondingly individualized. The figure of Old Ekdal is a case in point. In the first draft he is 'white-haired, meek ...' but in the play the word 'meek' is omitted and he enters wearing a 'dirty reddish-brown wig' which gives spice to the pathos of Hjalmar's declamations about the 'poor white-haired old man' and Relling's remark is added, 'Yes, tell me, — is it grey hair he has, or is it white?' The same process of contrast between individualization and generalization is applied to the setting, and while the minutest details of the scenery, such as the garret-doors and the mechanism of the net and sail-cloth, are carefully worked out, the actual locality, which in the earlier drafts was stated to be Kristiania, is finally not mentioned.

The same process is traceable in Ibsen's construction of the dialogue. In *Ghosts* we see Pastor Manders gradually being transformed from an open hypocrite to a cautious opportunist, and the development of the following snatch of dialogue is characteristic. In the first version Manders says (Act I): 'For if one *is* not unimpeachable one never attains one's object.' In the final manuscript this is transformed into: 'For if one is not *looked upon* as unimpeachable one never attains one's object.' Even this was caricaturing Manders too openly and Ibsen finally crossed out these words. In the early versions of *A Doll's House* Helmer is characterized descriptively by Nora to Mrs. Linde, but in the last version he reveals himself by his own discourse. When in the earlier version Helmer receives the letter from Krogstad he exclaims: 'Nora, you are saved.' In the final version this remark is changed to 'I am saved' and gives him away completely as a self-complacent egoist. Often as the play takes shape and the characters are transformed remarks are transferred from one character to another. For instance, in *Pillars of Society* the emancipated woman Lona Hessel, as the mouthpiece character, exclaims, 'You are blind to the existence of woman', giving the words more force than when the contrite villain Bernick in the fifth draft self-reproachfully says, 'We are blind to the existence of woman'.

It seems that Ibsen had no particularly rigid method of composition except the adherence to the principles of elimination, concentration and individualization. The theme and the original structure of the play were often abandoned and were superseded by stray ideas suggested by loose tags of conversation, newspaper advertisements or coincidences. The writing of *Pillars of Society* is a case in point. The first notes from 1870 foreshadow the theme which throughout is prominent in the play, that of the position of women in society, but this is finally relegated to a position of subordinate importance and is replaced by the broader question of truth and uprightness in society regardless of sex. The ironical title *Pillars of Society* was originally adopted without any irony at all, and the original villains were the open enemies of society, not those who hypocritically pretended to be pillars of society for their own personal gain. Bernick, the future hypocrite, is originally not portrayed as such, and is described as having 'a scorn for the ideal, which he vents chiefly against his wife, because she provokes him most'.

Ibsen's notes bear out his reliance on inspirations of the moment to form the basis of a play. He seems to have spent months making stray jottings and not bothering about connecting them. In his earlier plays the notes are sparse, due perhaps to the fact that he preferred not to write down his impressions but to keep them in his head instead. Also he was afraid of being spied on. His fury knew no bounds when his wife once picked up part of an envelope he had dropped in a train and read the word 'doctor' scrawled across it. Later in life he used notebooks and loose sheets of paper. The notebooks revealing the plans of *Hedda Gabler* are a sign of failing memory and that need for concentrated thought and absence of distraction which he mentions in the letter to Brandes (November 10th, 1886). Previously the only clues to his earliest plans are scraps of paper and backs of telegram forms. As he finally evolved the play from the plans he would write uninterrupted, making alterations of names and relationships and characters as he progressed. In the drafts of *Rosmersholm* Rosmer changes his name five times. He is first 'he', then 'S', then Boldt-Römer, then Rosenhjelm, then Rosmer. Rebekka in an early note is 'She', the governess of Rosmer's daughters, then 'Miss B', then 'Miss Radeck', then she becomes Agate, Rosmer's wife; in Act II she changes to Miss Dankert and in the following act she at last becomes Miss Rebekka West. The play itself develops in the same haphazard way. It was originally inspired by ideals of aristocratic liberalism and scorn of conservatism after the experiences of a summer in Norway. Ibsen then suddenly became disillusioned about the liberals, the play turned into a revelation of base political intrigue in the two opposing camps, and the aristocrat was transformed into the tragic victim instead of the triumphant hero. A critical spirit of contradiction seems to control the composition of Ibsen's plays, just as the plays themselves seem to grow out of a desire to contradict the plays that have preceded. *Ghosts* crushes all the ideals that had inspired *Pillars of Society* and *A Doll's House*, in *The Wild Duck* Relling upholds ideals as a stimulating fiction; truth triumphs over the past in *The Lady from the Sea*, but all the last plays except *Little Eyolf* demonstrate from various angles the impossibility for an individual to overcome a sick conscience.

As far as one can reconstruct the process from the available manuscripts, Ibsen wrote his plays very much in the way that he described to Jaeger. His drafts were never quite as regular as he imagined, sometimes we find five, sometimes only one, and many of his notes contain the germs of several and not of a single play. It was all in fact a very haphazard affair following a few simple constructive principles, aided by vision and imagination and impelled by an inspiration which was fed by anger, revenge or frustrated affection.

CHAPTER II

IBSEN'S ASSOCIATION WITH THE STAGE

IN concluding a study of Ibsen, Henning Kehler makes the following statement: 'Basically identical with ideas and clothed in a realism that never completely becomes flesh and blood, their fate is unreal and Ibsen's characters are at heart the products of a romantic poet's mind.' What is here said with reference to Ibsen's characters may be considered to apply to his drama as a whole. His early work, which marked him as a poet for life and in which we find all the themes which are varied and developed in his later plays and poems, is both in form and content the product of European and Scandinavian romanticism. And though his form develops with time, the content of his work remains largely static and consists in a repetition of romantic themes. While the main themes of Ibsen's work are romantic, such as his individualism, his revolt against society, his cult of ideal love, his worship of freedom and truth and his insistence on the individual's loyalty to his calling and mission, the features which are most salient in the development of his technique show a continual progress towards an illusion of realism with which to present his romantic characters and themes to the public of his day. Before examining the various particular aspects of his technique let us first trace the general outline of its development.

In one of his earliest criticisms from the year 1851 Ibsen wrote: 'In the realms of art, pure reality has no place, but on the contrary illusion.' To this principle he remains true throughout his life, and all his changes in technique are brought about with the intention of creating the greatest possible illusion according to the demands of the time. His technique develops in line with his experience as a practical theatre manager, and it is significant that it only attains complete individuality when Ibsen leaves Norway and is no longer restricted by conforming to the requirements of an out-of-date stage or of bigoted conservative directors. In contact with new movements in the European theatre Ibsen was able first of all to write for a new type of stage and later, as he developed, to refuse to write stage plays at all because the stage and actors no longer satisfied his demands for illusion. Throughout his period of voluntary exile abroad he repeatedly refused to return to Norway and direct the Christiania Theatre because the building and the management of the theatre did not conform to his demands. In later life his attitude to the stage became so pessimistic that he avoided going to theatres altogether. This shows how his artistic sensibility realized that, as a result of his long inexperience of the practical stage, his technique had out-distanced developments in the theatre and had progressed along a course which the theatre itself was not destined to follow. Just when his technique attained its highest perfection, the realistic peep-show stage became a thing of the past and theatre architects under the influence of the Elizabethans and the Greeks began to construct buildings for the revival of poetic drama in all its varying forms, ranging from the mass spectacle to the Kammerspiel. The opening of the National Theatre in Christiania in 1899, built on the traditional lines of the Italian opera house with its galleries and boxes and picture stage, was the sadly belated realization of a plan which Ibsen had advocated thirty years earlier, a building which neither complied with the structural demands of the European stage nor was fit for the production of the greatest works by Norway's most distinguished dramatist. In order to follow this course of development let us examine shortly Ibsen's relation to the stage and the repertoire of his time.

Ibsen's association with the theatre began at a very early age. In his childhood he was fascinated by the travelling companies of actors, chiefly Danish, which he saw in Skien, the conjurors and jugglers of the fairs, and above all the peep shows. In imitation of the latter he painted and cut out a series of paper figures representing his stage heroes and arranged them into tableaux. He was also an enthusiastic illusionist and once he gave a performance of self-invented conjuring tricks before an audience of friends and relations with the help of a younger brother whom he had concealed beneath the table. The latter subsequently betrayed the secret, to Ibsen's life-long consternation. His father's bankruptcy, and the family's retreat to the farm Venstøp outside Skien, cut Ibsen off from the outside world at the early age of eight, until he took up his work as an apothecary's apprentice in Grimstad. His time at Venstøp was spent mostly alone in the attic among the lumber left behind by the former tenant Nils Jørgen Hirschholm, an old sea-captain known as 'the flying Dutchman' who inspired the fancy of the lonely boy. Here he continued painting and cutting out figures and copying the pictures in the strange books he discovered there. Just before his sixteenth birthday, after being confirmed, he left home to take up his position as apothecary's assistant at Grimstad. Here he was abjectly poor and was unable to afford the solace of watching theatrical performances. He contented himself, however, with creating dramatic situations in the life around him by circulating epigrams about the leading people of the town. But while reading Cicero's Catiline orations and Sallust's *Catiline* for the entrance examination to Oslo University he found at last matter which satisfed his desire for dramatic effect, and, without any previous experience of the stage, wrote, during his hours of liberty at night, his first play *Catilina*. This he read as he progressed to his two friends Due and Schulerud, and the latter took the finished manuscript with him to Oslo and published it himself at his own expense in 1850, after repeated refusals by publishers to take the risk. This was just before Ibsen's arrival in the town. The Christiania Theatre politely refused to produce the play and it in fact never came on the stage until 1881, when Ludwig Josephson produced it in Stockholm. But the refusal of the play had the salutary effect of at last bringing Ibsen into contact with practical theatrical conditions.

When Ibsen arrived in Oslo the theatre was a stronghold of the Danish-minded public of the town, and a year after his arrival the Dane, Borgaard, with whom Ibsen was continually to cross swords, became director of the theatre. The history of the Norwegian theatre up to that date was that of a struggle between the Norwegian nationalists and the leading society of Oslo, which continued Danish fashions in dress and deportment and drama. Ibsen was himself to be instrumental in bringing this struggle to a triumphal conclusion for the nationalist party.

Up till 1810 theatrical life in Norway had depended entirely on amateur performances and the performances of travelling Danish companies. In 1810 J. P. Strömberg, the son of a Swedish tobacco merchant in Stockholm, obtained a royal privilege to open a theatre. In 1827 the first official town theatre in Oslo was opened under his management, but a year later, owing to financial difficulties, he handed over his directorship to a Dane, Jens Lang Bøcher. The actors were for the most part Danes, interspersed with a few Norwegians, and all efforts at forming a Norwegian school of dramatic art had failed. The repertoire consisted entirely of foreign plays except for the works of Holberg. Among the dramatists favoured were Oehlenschlæger, Schiller, Shakespeare, Beaumarchais, Lessing and Sheridan. In 1837 Bøcher, who had failed to improve Strömberg's finances, left and Strömberg sold the theatre to a Danish actor Saabye. National sentiment was rising in Norway and found its spokesman in the warm-hearted, naive and bombastic poet Wergeland, full of the spirit of the July revolution and paternal in his desire to lead and enlighten his people. One of his greatest triumphs was to be celebrated on the stage. In 1831 he attacked the theatre with its Danish actors and repertoire in a scathing article in *Morgenbladet*. His criticism was mainly directed against the Danish author Henrik Hertz, who was a popular vaudeville writer according to the prescriptions of Scribe, and the Danish aesthetician, philosopher and man of the world J. L. Heiberg. Welhaven, who represented Danish taste in Norway, mocked at Wergeland, maintaining that his campaign was only an expression of bitterness for the poverty of Norwegian literature and for the poor reception given to his own dramatic efforts.

In 1835, much to Wergeland's glee, the theatre was burnt to the ground, so money was collected for building a new theatre on Bankpladsen. In spite of Wergeland's hopes the new theatre was as before filled with Danish actors. But some consolation was offered by the management, who inaugurated a competition for the best Norwegian play to be performed at the opening. The play chosen for the celebrations in October 1837 was *Kong Sverres Ungdom* by A. Munch, an adherent of the Welhaven party. But a sop was thrown to Wergeland in that the management also found his play *Campbellerne* worthy to be produced. On the occasion of the second performance on January 28th, 1838, his opponents appeared in force and hissed the play. He had the satisfaction, however, of seeing his own supporters shout down the Danish party by their applause and finally throw them out of the theatre with physical force. This triumph Wergeland declared to be the greatest moment of his life, but it was of small consequence as far as the theatre was concerned, and the Danish personnel continued to enjoy patronage.

But the February revolution of 1848 set a new stream of nationalism flowing in Norway. The Soirée held in honour of Norwegian music, painting and poetry on March 28th, 1849, is in a way the culmination of nationalistic efforts in the 'forties,

All the Norwegian artists who had returned home owing to upheavals abroad met here to celebrate the regeneration of Norwegian culture, with the violinist and Utopian dreamer Ole Bull at their head. A year afterwards, before sailing for America to found his idyllic colony, he realized one of his nationalist dreams by opening Norway's first national stage in Bergen on January 2nd, 1850.

When Ibsen came to Oslo, however, the theatre was still dominated by Danes. The refusal of *Catilina* led him to investigate the requirements of the theatre for his future benefit. The repertoire was composed of high-sounding historical tragedies on Nordic themes, in slavish imitation of Oehlenschlæger, together with light vaudevilles in the manner of Heiberg and Hertz and the avowed master Scribe. *Catilina* came under neither of these headings, and Ibsen immediately began to conform to the taste of his public in his next play, *The Warrior's Barrow* (*Kjæmpehøjen*). This was accepted by the theatre and produced for the first time on September 26th, 1850, to survive three successful performances. Ibsen was praised by the critics and, most important of all, was given a free ticket to the theatre which he could now study to his heart's content, without considering the meagre resources of his pocket. Now he was able to learn something of a play's effectiveness on the stage, and witnessed performances of the then reigning masters of stage technique, Heiberg, Hertz and Scribe. The result of his observations was to begin work on a national romantic play *The Ptarmigan of Justedal* (*Rypen i Justedal*). The play was in four acts, but only the manuscripts of the first two survive. From the fragment that remains it is easy to see that the result of study as a spectator had given his technique and dialogue an ease which was not to be found in the stilted heroics of his first two plays. The stage directions show an attention to setting and scenery which was absent before.

It was in 1851 that Ibsen became co-editor with A. O. Vinje and Botten-Hansen of a satirical periodical, *Andhrimmer*, and in the articles which he wrote in this paper as dramatic critic we find the first indications of his conception of dramatic technique. His criticism of Gutzkow's *Zopf und Schwert* indicates a strongly nationalistic bias, but his theory is belied by his subsequent practice. He hails it as the first German play to break the artificial tradition of the French and Danish repertoire which dominated the Christiania stage, contrasts the French stress on situation with the German insistence on psychology as the basis of drama, and speaks scornfully of 'Scribe and Co.'s dramatic sweetmeats'. It was however in direct imitation of Scribe's intrigue technique that he wrote his next plays and as late as 1861 we find him defending the stage effectiveness of Scribe's work against the theorists, who, like himself ten years previously, had, in opposition to French taste, set up the less dramatic character drama of Germany as a paragon. (*The two Theatres in Christiana*, April 12th, 1861.) But while on the one hand he showed his antagonism to French repertoire, which appealed to the taste of the upper-class patrons of the theatre, he also stood out firm against the exaggerated forms of national operetta represented by such works as P. A. Jensen's *The Fairy's Home*, which was calculated to draw an audience among patriotic intellectuals and the lower middle classes, with its hotchpotch of folk-song lyrics, its medley of national costumes, country dances and games, and its picturesquely inaccurate provincial setting — all held together with a feeble plot laid on long-lost children, recognitions and improbable revelations.

Ibsen's most constructive ideas are, however, to be found in the newspaper published by the Studenter-Samfundet (*Samfundsbladet*). Here he evolved a plan for the creation of a specifically Norwegian theatre free from foreign influences, the actors of which were to be recruited among the Norwegian students. This idea was realized shortly afterwards when the Norwegian dramatic school was founded. He also curiously enough dwelt at length on such an unimportant form of drama as the vaudeville. But it must be remembered that the great Danish literary pundit and playwright J. L. Heiberg, who had introduced Hegelian philosophy to Scandinavia, had succeeded in proving, by a specious form of Hegelian dialectics, that the vaudeville was the most suitable form of dramatic art for the stage of the day. It is these ideas we hear re-echoed in Ibsen's article *The Hostel in Greenland* and they are here applied to a special form of vaudeville, namely the student vaudeville, the great exponent of which was the Dane Hostrup. The recurring themes involved the repeated conflict of the student and the philistine, a point on which Ibsen lays much stress, and it is interesting to note how two of Ibsen's plays, *Midsummer Eve* and *Love's Comedy*, reflect a repetition of similar conflicts and a similar grouping of characters. This is only one instance of the way in which Ibsen adapted a popular form of drama to his particular needs.

His activities as dramatic critic were concluded at the end of the year, when on November 6th, 1851, he was appointed as a salaried dramatist at Ole Bull's Norwegian Theatre in Bergen. In February 1852 he was granted a travelling scholarship by the theatre to study the stage in Denmark and Germany, with the prospect of becoming stage manager and producer on his return. The subsequent analysis of Ibsen's technique shows what an important part this tour played in his development, in broadening his vision and in giving him a sense of stage effect which his earlier plays and critical articles entirely ignore. His nationalistic antagonism to French intrigue drama was overcome, and the intrigue technique of the plays he now wrote is a tacit acknowledgment of his debt to 'Scribe and Co.' He saw Shakespeare performed in Copenhagen and Dresden and he read with profit Hermann Hettner's book *Das moderne Drama* (1852). He seems particularly to have been impressed by his eulogy of Scribe and his analysis of Shakespeare's historical plays.

The result of his experiences on this tour is to be found in the records of his activities as producer and dramatist in Bergen, and they will be treated in detail later. They may roughly be divided into three categories: practical production, practical playwriting and dramatic theory. He transferred to the small Bergen stage the mechanical devices and scenic effects which he had studied abroad. But his tour took place at an unfortunate date in the history of the technical development of stage apparatus. Stages were still being set with two dimensional scenery arranged as flies, wings and flats behind one another and skilfully painted so as to give the illusion of solidity and perspective, an illusion which was sadly broken by the presence of the actor, who failed to conform to the rapid changes of dimension as he walked up and down stage. Both the Copenhagen and Dresden theatres still used these settings, and Ibsen transposed their practice on to the Bergen stage, having failed to follow up H. C. Andersen's recommendation to visit the Burg Theater in Vienna, where he might have learnt a very different technique. However, such flats painted in perspective were cheap and well within the means of the Bergen theatre's finances. This type of setting largely explains why Ibsen never fought shy of grandiose scenery for his earlier romantic plays, while his transition to the technique of realistic illusion coincides with his adoption of the indoor setting, and of the indoor setting of domestic proportions where the actors were not out of perspective. These latter enclosed settings are a striking contrast to the open scenery of Ibsen's years of apprenticeship, when the side walls were placed as wings behind one another and doors were never used except as decorations; windows, curtains and draperies were all painted in the flat and even superfluous furniture was cut out in painted cardboard screens, while often other 'props' lacked plastic form, and such objects as loaves and dishes and cheese and puddings were represented by two dimensional cardboard models. What was true of scenery was also true of the costumes, and expense was saved by the use of paper and cardboard and tinsel and silver paper for making uniforms, armour and weapons, so that Ibsen never had to take such extravagances into consideration while writing. Never perhaps was he ever more able than in Bergen to be true to his maxim that 'in the realms of art pure reality has no place, but on the contrary illusion'. It was only the realization that the illusion was becoming insufficient that led him to his conventional realistic technique.

Since the plays will be examined in detail subsequently there is no need to dwell on them here at any length. Let it be sufficient to say that he succeeded in fulfilling his duties as salaried dramatist in Norway's first national theatre by writing four nationalist plays (*Midsummer Eve, Lady Inger of Østråt, The Feast at Solhaug, Olaf Liljekrans*) in which national themes were presented with a fair semblance of accurate local colour and a style that ranged from poetic measured prose to imitation ballad and folk-song verse. They differed from their prototypes in Norway by being constructed with awareness for stage effect, in a jigsaw puzzle of situations, surprises, secrets, revelations, reconciliations and retributions which seem primitive to-day but which mark a new departure in Norwegian drama. In spite of the artificiality of these plays they have their merits, and Ibsen realized this when he revised *Lady Inger of Østråt* and *The Feast at Solhaug* and published them again in later life as a contribution to his unceasing efforts to demonstrate the consistency of his development as a dramatist from the very beginning. In *Lady Inger* we see how Ibsen had profited by his study of intrigue drama, and not only in the heroine's likeness to Lady Macbeth, but also in the diction and atmosphere of

40

the whole play we find numerous reminiscences of Shakespeare. A year after writing the play he read a paper to a literary society in Bergen on Shakespeare and his influence on Nordic art. (The Society of 22nd December; November 27th, 1855.) The paper has unfortunately not been preserved but it no doubt contained indirect acknowledgments of Ibsen's own indebtedness to Shakespeare. The influence of Shakespeare was particularly important in Ibsen's treatment of history in his plays. Hettner in *Das moderne Drama* had spoken of Shakespeare's art of presenting the spirit of history by subordinating detail to character and dramatic effect, the very method pursued by Ibsen in all his historical dramas up to *Emperor and Galilean*, his 'world historical play'. In the year in which he wrote *The Warriors of Helgeland*, a historical play and at the same time Ibsen's first conscious attempt at realism, he attacked Thiele's play *Thyre Boløxe* because it sacrificed dramatic effect to pedantic historical accuracy. At the same time he praised A. Munch's drama *Lord William Russell* because it conformed to his ideas of what a historical play should be. He sums up his remarks in the following words: 'We have no real right to demand the facts of history from the true historical play, but rather its possibilities, not the persons and characters demonstrated by history, but the spirit and thought of the time.' Here again we cannot but call to mind Ibsen's early insistence on art as illusion.

These latter articles were written when Ibsen had already left Bergen in the autumn of 1857 and had become artistic director of the Norwegian Theatre in Christiania. This theatre had been founded in 1852 as a dramatic school and was inspired with a desire to outdistance the Bergen theatre in its demand for nationalism in language and repertoire. Ibsen came to Oslo with double the salary he had received in Bergen and he was filled with high hopes of reviving Norwegian drama. But his enthusiasm was soon crushed. The theatre when he took it over was weighed down with heavy debts for the liquidation of which Ibsen was answerable to the board of directors. In order to reduce this debt he was forced to renounce his artistic ideals and to give the public a repertoire of Danish and French vaudevilles and farces, which were also the only type of drama for which his mediocre company of actors were suited. Before very long he had to accept the Norwegian Theatre as a second rate institution, as is shown by the fact that he first offered his own play *The Warriors of Helgeland* to the Dane

41

Borgaard of the Christiania Theatre before producing it on his own stage. In spite of Ibsen's efforts the theatre went bankrupt in the summer of 1862, and in 1863 an amalgamation was brought about with the Christiania Theatre, to which Ibsen was appointed as artistic adviser.

The years of his directorship were the most painful of his life and the most sterile as far as literary production is concerned. (He only wrote two more plays, *Love's Comedy* and *The Pretenders*, before he left Norway in 1864, though many of his famous longer poems date from this period.) He lived under continual financial stress, and, but for the presence of his wife, whom he married in 1858, he might well have succumbed to the illnesses and thoughts of suicide which beset him. His distress was largely a result of a conflict which looms large in his subsequent work, the conflict between the ideals of art and the practical demands of life. As artist and as practical theatre manager he was attacked from all sides. The directors of the theatre accused him of idleness, the actors questioned his capacity as a producer, the audiences complained that he was too high-brow when he tried to live up to his ideals of poetic drama, and his opponents at the Christiania Theatre scoffed when he was compelled for material reasons to resort to the Danish-French repertoire which he so abhorred. When his play *The Warriors of Helgeland* was refused by the Dane Borgaard, the artistic director of the Christiania Theatre, Ibsen inaugurated the final conflict between the Norwegian nationalists and the Danophiles. This ended in 1863 with the return of all but six Danish actors to Denmark and the partial realization of Ibsen's demands for a Norwegian stage in the reorganization of the Christiania Theatre. In a reasoned series of articles which he wrote in 1861 he based his demands for a national stage on a relation of the factors involved in dramatic illusion to time, race and local taste. He had no complaints to make against the actors or repertoire of the Christiania Theatre, except in so far as they were Danish and appealed only to the prosperous, cultivated classes. He called it a bastard theatre, which might do very well in Copenhagen, but which in Christiania was quite as anomalous as the company of French actors which performed in the town during the reign of Christian VII and played exclusively to the Danish officials, nobles and persons of the upper classes, only admitting *bourgeois* into the auditorium when there chanced to be tickets to spare. He also defended himself on the score of producing trivial plays by declaring it a sign of inferior culture on the part of the public to demand the production of classical masterpieces for which the actors and stage conditions were not suited and which they themselves did not genuinely appreciate. He concluded with the statement that it is better to put on good productions of inferior plays which are within the scope of the actors and the comprehension of the public than to continue to produce masterpieces badly.

Ibsen's efforts to make a success of the theatre as he found it were a dismal failure and this contributed to the sum of grievances which drove him, romantic idealist as he was, to search for fame and fortune in foreign lands. He poured out all his suppressed anger and bitterness in the two revengeful epic plays *Brand* and *Peer Gynt*, which he never intended for the stage, and then set out as a dramatist, untrammelled by the organization or apparatus of any existing theatre, to write plays for a stage which existed only in his imagination. This imaginary stage was the result of painful years of experience and the fullest realization of his demands for dramatic illusion, which had been shipwrecked in practice under the pressure of intrigue and financial strain. After leaving Norway in 1864 he steadily refused to have anything to do with the directorship of any theatre, though he received repeated offers. He made certain practical demands regarding the structure and administrative organization of the theatre. They never were accepted, and he never managed another theatre for the rest of his life. But his interest in the practical stage remained to the end of his days and was important in influencing his technique.

Three months after Ibsen's departure from Norway, in July 1864, the management of the Christiania Theatre offered him the post of artistic director. Bjørnson had refused to accept the post unless his powers as director were to be extended at the expense of the managing committee. His requests were refused and Ibsen was offered the post under the old conditions. What was not good enough for Bjørnson was not good enough for him and he refused point blank without even making conditions. In 1870 the post of director was again offered to Ibsen. He refused again and proposed Bjørnson. The management would not accept him, and the majority of actors left the theatre and set up a rival concern for a period of three years under Bjørnson's leadership. During his

43

visit to Christiania in 1874 Ibsen spent much time with the new manager of the theatre, the Swede, Ludwig Josephson. The latter had done much to modernize the organization of the theatre and had extended its activities by the introduction of opera, a fact that subsequently brought about his fall. Ibsen admired his efforts to widen the scope of the theatre, and, when in 1875 the management and the press began to intrigue against him, Ibsen wrote him a letter, thanking him for all he had done in introducing his work to the stage. He promised him that the present difficulties were merely transitory and that better times were approaching, hinting also at the possibility of the construction of a larger theatre. The year following Ibsen wrote to Josephson promising him active help in his difficulties with the management, proposing to write a series of articles in a Norwegian paper and insisting that above all it was necessary to change the antiquated form of committee directorship. His articles were never published, if they were ever written, for Josephson was forced to resign in 1877. In a letter to Hartvig Lassen (November 2nd, 1877) he vituperates against the system of committee management. 'The management,' he writes, 'would have acted more in the interest of the theatre, if, instead of doing away with the intendant and the opera, it had done away with itself. The theatre will never establish itself as long as it is managed by a committee. This principle is recognized all over the world; theatre-managements have been done away with everywhere except in Norway; that is why things are as they are up there.' Not only do his letters thirteen years after any practical experience of theatre management show an intimate acquaintance with the problems associated with such work, but from this period also there are preserved some notes which record constructive proposals for the building and administration of a new theatre in Christiania. These proposals may well have been intended for inclusion in the suggested articles on behalf of Josephson, and they show an intimate acquaintance with the financial problems and their partial solution according to European methods by the letting of shops and café on the ground floor, together with a restaurant above in the theatre foyer. Ibsen had learnt much during his years abroad from the theatres with which he was acquainted in Germany, and one cannot accuse him of being out of contact with the material concerns of the stage.

In 1884 Bjørnson again tried to persuade Ibsen to take over the

Henrik Ibsen

Ibsen at the age of thirty

Ibsen in the early 1870s

directorship of the Christiania Theatre. Ibsen acknowledged he was tempted, but, remembering the old conflicts between his work as a dramatist and his activities as theatre manager, he decided that his work as a dramatist came first and that he would not stake his steady income from writing against the improbable eventuality of making a livelihood as a theatre manager without coming to blows with the managing committee. He again insisted on the necessity of having a modern theatre building in Christiania, repeating it in a letter to *Dagbladet* with the words: 'It is a crime against our talented and capable actors and against our national dramatic literature, to support such a wretched organization in the old out-of-date building, without contributions either from the state or the municipality. I shall not implicate myself in such a crime.' This was the last time Ibsen ever took any active part in polemics about the theatre, but when in 1899 the National Theatre was opened he was hailed together with Bjørnson as one of those who had rendered possible the belated realization of this ideal in theatre architecture, which came some thirty years after its time.

CHAPTER III

THE DEVELOPMENT OF IBSEN'S TECHNIQUE

FROM this examination of Ibsen's contact with the theatre after leaving Norway arise several points which are of significance for his technique. We see that as late as 1884, twenty years after association with the stage, Ibsen was thinking in the terms of a particular type of theatre. This disproves the general assumption that he only succeeded in perfecting his realistic technique by cutting adrift from the theatre altogether. He did, it is true, dissociate himself from the stage, but only in so far as it represented for him a type of repertoire, a standard of acting and a method of management which was not in agreement with his ideals of dramatic illusion. His last refusal to become an active theatre man was a matter of policy. He knew the theatre could not pay if the administration were not changed and he knew that he was the last person to be accepted by conservative managers. He became pessimistic about the theatre, and after 1884 we see his technique developing along lines which ask the impossible of dramatic presentation. A contemporary critic complained that Ibsen no longer wrote to be acted, but to be read, that a play like *Hedda Gabler* was too full of psychological subtleties to be dramatic and should have been written as a novel. This line of development can be most easily traced in the settings and stage directions which become more and more detailed.

As his technique developed, he also freed himself from the convention of the interior setting which he had set up in his earlier modern social plays. With *The Lady from the Sea* his plays expand into the open air. The interior setting had been a result of a reaction against the unnatural perspectives of outdoor scenery and the conviction that full illusion is alone possible by means of concentration and simplification. It was a conviction that had resulted from his experience as a producer on an indifferent stage and which he had expressed in 1861, when he spoke of the merit of producing inferior plays well rather than masterpieces badly. But when he was no longer reckoning in the terms of a particular type of theatre, and when he became acquainted with the resources of modern theatre apparatus, he abandoned the interior setting. But in the later outdoor settings he avoided unnatural perspective scenery, always keeping his characters on the same plane, within the confines of a garden, behind a fence, or on a bank or slope which backed the stage with a near horizon. This restricted the movements of the actors within the bounds of an ordinary-sized room, leaving the back cloth behind to complete the illusion of space. The last scene in *John Gabriel Borkman*, where Borkman and Ella walk away from the house through the forest, presupposes the use of a moving or revolving stage and scenery, a concession to developments in stage machinery which would never have been dared in earlier years. Here we find Ibsen using a technical device in his old age for which he had not provided in his plans for theatre construction twenty years before.

But in spite of this last isolated instance of his consideration for stage apparatus (another explanation of this scene might equally well be that he had not thought of the stage at all) Ibsen was definitely antagonistic to the stage in his later years. He never went to see his plays performed, and he was the despair of producers when they persuaded him to help with rehearsals. When, at the request of Felix Philippi, he assisted with the production of *Rosmersholm* in Germany, he drove the actress playing Rebekka's part to distraction by his abuse and then gave the whole matter up as hopeless, turned his back on the stage, hiding his face in his hands and mumbling imprecations to himself for the rest of the rehearsal. On another occasion he expressed his disgust and abomination at the largeness of Frau Ramlo's hands in spite of her magnificent acting of Nora. He seemed, like Gordon Craig, to feel the actors as intruders between himself and his work, and it is significant that his stage directions made it even harder for them to live up to his requirements. The only instance of Ibsen's interest in the stage during his later life was when he supervised the production of *Little Eyolf* for its first performance in Oslo, but then he gave the impression of regarding the stage and the actors as an unavoidable inconvenience which it was his duty out of politeness to tolerate.

Gordon Craig, in speaking of Ibsen, said: 'Realism is only exposure, where art is revelation.' We remember Ibsen's romantic insistence in 1851 on illusion and not realism as the basis of art, and we find him consistent in theory as well as in practice in his later so-called realistic work. After reading Bjørnson's *Newly Weds* in 1866 he wrote: 'This is the way in which modern drama must take shape in our country.' Bjørnson returned home from Paris in 1863 full of enthusiasm for the developments of the modern problem drama in France, and Ibsen's approval of *Newly Weds* has often been accepted as an indirect appreciation of the French *pièce à thèse*. As early as 1857 Ibsen, in an essay on the actor A. V. Wiehe, condemned this form of drama, which he called a 'treatise on social conditions — in dramatic form'. Connecting this latter statement with his appreciation of Bjørnson's play we are compelled to find here not an appreciation of the French *pièce à thèse* in Norwegian clothing, but an appreciation of the play on its own merits founded more than likely on its dissimilarity to the work of Augier and Dumas fils. Bjørnson here succeeded in treating a modern social problem in a modern dress of character and dialogue under the acknowledged influence of Alfred de Musset. While Ibsen never failed to revile Dumas, he professed admiration for de Musset, which for Ibsen was far on the way to an acknowledgment of indebtedness. Refuting Jules Lemaître's charges of plagiarism Ibsen wrote to Brandes in 1896 the following lines: 'To Alexandre Dumas I owe nothing at all as far as dramatic form is concerned — except the fact that I have learnt from his plays how to avoid various rather reprehensible mistakes and blunders of which he is not seldom guilty.' This is a fairly conditional denial which may be accepted as far as technique and form are concerned. It does not exclude the borrowing of themes, and there seems to be no doubt that Dumas's romantic idealization of free-love and Augier's variations on the conflict between money and affection fuelled the moral fire of Ibsen's work. But of other French dramatists next to Scribe, he was most appreciative of Alfred de Musset, and it is significant that in 1870, long after he had begun to react consciously against Scribe, he wrote to his publisher thanking him for sending a copy of a play which he commends as reminding him of 'the manner of Alfred de Musset's ''proverbes'' and especially of Bjørnson's *Newly Weds*'. This throws a new light on Ibsen's appreciation of Bjørnson's play in 1866, and is important as a symptom of his attitude to realism in modern social drama. He conceived it then, as we see from his subsequent practice, as a means of pointing a moral. This was administered, for the sake of illusion, in the form of a charade by cultivated persons, conversing in everyday language, somewhat epigrammatic it is true, but dressed in the clothes of the time and set in a homely *milieu* familiar to everybody. Ibsen had frequently produced de Musset's *Un caprice* in earlier days and his admiration for his artistry remained. There is no doubt that his earliest hopes for a modern Norwegian drama were based on a continuation of the somewhat artificial but supremely artistic de Musset manner.

But at this time (1866) Ibsen was occupied with the last of his indignation dramas in verse, which were far from being attempts at realism and were not intended for stage production. When, however, in 1867 he wrote to Bjørnson, enraged at Clemens Petersen's criticism of *Peer Gynt*, he exclaimed: 'My book is poetry; and if it is not, it shall be. The conception of poetry will in our country, Norway, have to suit itself to my book.' And later he added: 'I am, however, pleased with the injustice that has been done me: I see God's help and providence therein; for I can feel my strength growing as I get angrier. If there is to be war, then so be it! If I am not a poet, then I have nothing to lose. I will try my hand as a photographer. All my contemporaries up there in Norway I shall deal with singly, one person at a time as I have done with the chauvinists in the language question; I shall not spare the child in the mother's womb, nor the thoughts or emotions concealed in the words of a single individual who merits the honour of being included.' True to his word, Ibsen never wrote a verse drama again, and with his next play lived up to his threat to become a photographer of his contemporaries, or perhaps rather to pose as a photographer, for it is just this illusion of photographic realism which stamps him as such a profound artist. In 1869 he wrote his first modern drama in prose, the satirical comedy, *The League of Youth*, and though the plot is built in the old intrigue style, ending with revelations, retribution and three happy engagements, the dialogue and characterization give an illusion of everyday reality which is the modern counterpart of the realistic local colour in his later historical plays. In a letter to Brandes while writing the play he mentions the strong realistic colouring of his work and speaks with pride of his successful elimination of monologues and asides. There is no doubt that the realism and objectivity of the dialogue were in a large measure due to Brandes's criticism of his play, *The Pretenders*. Ibsen in his letter acknowledges the debt with the words: 'Your fully justified accusation regarding the clumsy interpolation of speeches by the author in *The Pretenders* has had its effect.' In the criticism of the play, written in 1867, Brandes had complained that Ibsen allowed 'the characters to express themselves in far too general terms, too well calculated and suited to a thousand situations, just at moments when they ought to be imagined to be exclusively occupied with what is happening to them personally, to them alone, in that particular situation'. As one instance he gave Ingebjørg's words: 'It is the lot of woman to love, to sacrifice everything and to be forgotten.' In the second edition Ibsen altered the phrase: 'It is the lot of woman' to 'it has been my lot'. Always in his later works, beginning with *The League of Youth*, he avoided the use of phrases which were of general and not particular application, thus progressing a step beyond the influence of de Musset whose 'proverbes' were based on the demonstration of a general maxim. Ibsen expressed his opinion on the question of objectivity in dialogue again during the storm which raged after the publication of *Ghosts*, when he wrote to Sophus Schandorph (January 6th, 1882) and condemned the whole affair as a slight against his technique and artistry. 'People', he wrote, 'try to make me responsible for the opinions which are expressed by individual characters in the drama. And yet there is not a single sentence, not a single utterance in the whole book for which the author is answerable. I took good care to guard against such a possibility. The particular method, the kind of technique which is the basis for the form of the book, naturally forbade that the author should appear in the dialogue. My intention was to give the reader the impression that he was experiencing a piece of reality as he was reading. But nothing could counteract such intentions more effectively than the interpolation of the author's opinions into the dialogue. And don't people at home believe I have enough of a dramatist's critical sense to realize such a fact?' By 1882 this factor in his technique has become a fixed principle which he feels it reprehensible to question.

It is a significant coincidence that Ibsen's adoption of a realistic technique occurs simultaneously with an important change in his own life. He left Norway a poor and dejected man. In 1866 he achieved his first success with the publication of *Brand*. Financial security, social recognition and literary fame made of him a somewhat prim and self-complacent figure with habits that became increasingly more fixed. The same is the case with Ibsen's dramatic technique, which in these years finds its form, and becomes fixed with only the slightest developments of detail until the end of his life. It seems not improbable that Ibsen's personal approximation to type may have contributed to the tendency to abandon experiment and to standardize his technique.

Ibsen's apprenticeship to his new technique was spent in the writing of *Emperor and Galilean*. The play was published on October 16th, 1873, but its origin dates back as early as 1864. It is Ibsen's dullest play, but it is a remarkably conscientious achievement, and the technical skill with which he has treated the gigantic task of developing the action and manipulating the innumerable characters is nothing short of miraculous. He himself wrote of the play to his publisher: 'This play has been a Herculean task for me — not in its composition, which was easy, but in all the pains it has cost me to familiarize myself freshly and clearly with such distant and strange times.' It was the effort required to give an illusion of reality to the extensive historical sources he had examined that cost him all his time and trouble. When Gosse early in 1874 sent him his appreciation of the play and regretted that it had not been written in verse this touched Ibsen to the quick. He answered Gosse with the following words: '. . . the play, as you will have noticed, is presented in a most realistic form; the illusion I wished to create was one of reality; I wanted to give the reader the impression that what he was reading was something that had really happened. If I had used verse, I would have counteracted my own intentions and the task I had set myself. The numerous everyday insignificant characters I had purposely included in the play would have become undefined and confused with one another if I had allowed them all to speak in rhythmic beats. We no longer live in the days of Shakespeare, and amongst sculptors there is already talk of painting statues in natural colours. Much can be said for and against in the matter. I would not like to have Venus de Milo painted, but I would prefer to see a negro's head in black rather than white marble. In general the form of diction ought to conform to the degree of ideality which pervades the play. My new play is no tragedy in the old meaning of the word; what I have wanted to portray

51

is human beings and that is just why I did not want them to speak "the language of the gods".'

Ibsen here expresses his conviction that realism is a question of degree. A good measure of the degree of ideality in Ibsen's work is to be found in his attitude to the use of verse. He published an edition of his collected poems in 1871 and a second enlarged edition came out in 1875. In 1876 and 1882, however, a third and fourth edition appeared, with corrections but no additions. In a letter to Olaf Skavlan, refusing his invitation to contribute to a new periodical, he excused himself with the words: 'I do not write poems'. In May 1883 the Norwegian actress Lucie Wolf had written to Ibsen's wife to ask if he could be persuaded to write a prologue to celebrate her thirtieth anniversary on the stage. Ibsen replied in person and refused with the words: 'I cannot because of my conception of art. Prologues, epilogues and all such things ought to be unconditionally banished from the stage. Dramatic art alone belongs there; and declamation is not dramatic art. The prologue would naturally have to be written in verse; for that is the custom. But I cannot assist in the preservation of this custom. Verse has done acting considerable harm. An actor, who has his repertoire in contemporary drama, ought not to allow a line to pass his lips. Verse forms will scarcely be of any significance in the drama of the near future; for the poet's aims in the future will scarcely be compatible with them. They will in consequence decay. Artistic forms die out just as the fantastic animal forms of primeval times died out when their time was come.

'A tragedy in iambic pentameters is already to-day as rare a phenomenon as the dodo, of which only a few specimens still exist down on an African island.

'I myself during the last 7-8 years have scarcely written a single line, but have exclusively devoted myself to the incomparably harder task of writing poetry in straightforward realistic every-day language.'

Such an attitude is typical of the period during which Ibsen was so absorbed with the development of his new technique that he was blind to all other artistic forms. In June of the following year while occupied with the composition of *The Wild Duck* he wrote to Theodor Caspari and said: 'I certainly remember, that I once expressed myself disrespectfully with regard to verse; but that was a result of my own momentary attitude to that art form. I have long since ceased to set up principles of general application, because I no longer believe that such principles can be set up.' He wrote, as it happened, singularly few poems during the rest of his life (his next poem was written in 1886) but his tolerance of verse and other art forms begins at a time when he has attained complete mastery of his own technique and is able to look at it in detached objectivity. The plays which begin with *The Wild Duck* are consequently the ones which are most interesting to study from the technical point of view, because we are able to appreciate the infinite variations which Ibsen made in the rigid conventions which he imposed upon himself.

There are two outside factors which were of considerable importance in developing Ibsen's realistic technique: his connection with the Meiningen actors and his association with Brandes. Brandes played the double part of Ibsen's John the Baptist and his guardian angel in the critical years of his development as a dramatist. He prepared Ibsen's way with criticism and theory, and defended him valiantly in the storms that raged round his early social dramas. I have already mentioned how Brandes's criticism of *The Pretenders* was instrumental in the development of realistic dialogue in *The League of Youth*. In 1870 Ibsen received from his publisher a copy of Brandes's book *Criticisms and Portraits*. From his formal and laconic expression of thanks to Brandes it is hard to see whether he had read the book or no. But it is not unlikely that he sooner or later read the essay on Shakespeare's realism in which Brandes had discussed the technique of setting and characterization in *Henry IV*. He here attacked the current opinions emanating from Germany, that Shakespeare's drama was based on the enunciation of universal principles, the characters being conceived as abstract ideas. Brandes points to the flesh and blood realism with which Shakespeare presents his characters and says, in discussing Hotspur, that 'it is with a penetration and profound appreciation of eccentricities, defects, caprices, whims and habits, all a result of temperament, the swift or slow circulation of the blood, physique, life indoors or in the open, on horseback and in action, and with an affection for the smallest details that Shakespeare builds up his greatest, his most heroic characters. A nervous gait, stuttering speech, bad memory, absentmindedness, nothing is too insignificant for him. They portray themselves in every phrase they utter, without ever saying a word about themselves . . .' And so Brandes continues, describing the details of Shakespeare's description of *milieu* and all the accessories to the action. Ibsen was profoundly conscious of his lack of critical faculty, of his tendency to be blinded by the work he had in hand and he was very dependent on Brandes's judgment. He was himself much interested in Shakespeare and later in life praised Brandes's book on Shakespeare, which extended the ideas advanced in his first Shakespearean essay. There is probably a continuity of purpose linking this early essay with the detailed realistic technique with which Ibsen was then struggling in the composition of *Emperor and Galilean,* and the probability is increased by knowing that his early paper on Shakespeare alluded almost certainly to *Henry V,* a play to which Hettner had pointed as a model for the historical dramatist. Ten days after Ibsen read his paper the literary society invited some of the actors from the theatre to the celebrations of the society's tenth anniversary, and Johannes Brun afterwards entertained the company by recitations of the Falstaff scenes in *Henry V.* Ibsen's realism developed from the local colour realism of historical drama to the realistic *milieu* of his modern social plays.

Another factor in developing Ibsen's realistic technique may be found in his meeting with the Meiningen Company and their realistic production of historical plays. Duke George II of Saxe-Meiningen was responsible for one of the greatest theatrical reforms of the nineteenth century in Germany. He had received a liberal education, was a good draughtsman and painter and interested in the theatre. When in 1872 his second wife died he devoted most of his time to the theatre and in 1873 married the actress Ellen Franz. He was imbued with an antiquarian sense for historical accuracy in art which pursued him in his career as a theatre reformer. His tutor had been Professor Andreas Müller, the Düsseldorf painter, and with him he had undertaken a study tour in Italy. His significance in the German theatre is that he abolished star performances and with a sense of artistic proportion replaced them with ensemble acting. At the same time, however, he was influenced by the historical realism of the schools of English acting which were represented by Charles Kean, Macready and Phelps. He came into contact with the realistic movement on the one hand through Dingelstedt, the intendant of the Weimar court theatre, who was married to an English singer, and on the other from his own experience of seeing Phelps perform in Berlin in 1859. In the productions of the Meiningen Company we meet with the final consummation of this school of acting. The historical accuracy of costume was a question of great importance, as also the material and quality of the cloth, and Duke George was one of the founders of the study of historical fashion and dress on the stage. Scenery and setting were also reformed by him. He was unsparing in his pains to set his performances according to the minutest historical details; he used three dimensional scenery that was solid and firm and not prone to flap, and even used real trees and other realistic accessories, like Max Reinhart in later years. It was in 1876 that Ibsen first made the acquaintance of the Duke. In July the Meiningen Company produced *The Pretenders* in Berlin with great success, and for a week afterwards Ibsen was the guest of the Duke at his castle, Liebenstein. On his departure he was decorated with the Knight's Cross of the Ernestine Order 1st class, a compliment which more than anything would make this experience memorable. The date of his first meeting with the Meininger and their realistic technique is significant in that it precedes by a whole year the completion of Ibsen's first wholly realistic modern play, *Pillars of Society*. The setting and detail of the stage directions, with their reference to gesture and expression, could almost have been taken out of a Meiningen producer's manuscript, and the detailed realism of the play strikes one as a reminiscence of the Meininger and an exploitation of Meiningen methods in the interest of modern social drama. The influence of the Meiningen Company on Ibsen's technique cannot be proved, but circumstantial evidence goes to show that it was a factor contributing to the evolution of his pseudo-realism.

In 1884, during the composition of *The Wild Duck*, Ibsen consciously altered his technique. Together with the printer's manuscript he sent his publisher a letter in which he said: 'This new play occupies in a way a place by itself in my dramatic production; the method diverges in various aspects from my former practice. However, I will make no further pronouncements on that score. The critics I hope will find the points; anyhow they will find diverse matters for disagreement and diverse points to interpret. At the same time I hope *The Wild*

Duck perhaps may induce some of our younger dramatists to venture out in a new direction, and I would consider this most desirable.' So familiar had the critics become with Ibsen's manner that they were all unquestionably puzzled by the play. Ibsen here breaks with his problem play-writing and occupies himself exclusively with human psychology. The break marks a new departure in his technique of characterization, abandoning moral for psychological motivation. Hedvig's suicide is not brought about in order to illustrate a moral maxim. It is the result of a subtle chain of causes, half-uttered suggestions and innuendoes and thought-associations, which combine to affect her sensitive and affectionate nature. This form of technique is characteristic of all Ibsen's later plays, though in *The Lady from the Sea* and *Little Eyolf* it is covered with a layer of moral sophistry which breaks the illusion. In *Rosmersholm* he used the pretext of contemporary political questions for a great psychological drama, but this was the last time social problems appeared in his work.

In 1887, while he was evolving the themes of *The Lady from the Sea*, he made a speech in Gothenburg, and the report states 'that he appreciated the kindness with which he had been received all the more, since his polemical interests were now on the wane and that he felt his poetry to be progressing towards new forms'. His later plays, with the exception of *Hedda Gabler*, show an increasing dualism between realism and romanticism, and his technique of dialogue, setting and characterization displays a growing tendency to give commonplace reality a symbolical significance. This is particularly characteristic of the last autobiographical confession plays which begin with *The Master Builder*. When, in the third act of *John Gabriel Borkman*, John Gabriel makes for the door to go out into the storm he says: 'Out into the storm alone then! My hat! My coat!' and when Ella Rentheim asks him where he is going he gives his action a symbolical significance with the words: 'Out into the storm of life.' And in the last act of the same play, when old Foldal comes in limping after having been run over by the sleigh in which his daughter and Borkman's son are driving away with Mrs. Wilton, the very realistic accident is again treated symbolically. Ella tries to persuade Borkman to help Foldal into the house. He refuses and Ella exclaims: 'But listen, he has been run over.' 'Oh,' answers Borkman, 'we all have to be run over — sometime in our lives.' In *When We Dead*

Awaken we meet with similar instances. This type of symbolical realism is the outcome of the dictum which he had enunciated in 1851, namely that 'In the realms of art pure reality has no place, but on the contrary illusion'.

After finishing his life's work he wrote to his French translator Count Prozor in 1900, hinting that he might still continue to write, but that if he did so he would alter his technique and his themes. 'I do not yet know', he wrote, 'how far I shall be able to write a new play; but if I continue to preserve the intellectual and physical powers in which I still rejoice, I would not like to stay away from the old battlefields permanently. But if such were the case I would then come forward with new weapons and new equipment.' He was evidently contemplating a complete break with his old technique. What form it would have taken we do not know. But his development indicates that the poetic drama of the neo-romantics would have tempted him. He never realized his hopes, however, and a stroke robbed him of the health and vigour necessary to continue his work.

In the foregoing pages I have endeavoured to trace the development of Ibsen's attitude towards the question of dramatic illusion, and to indicate the lines along which he individualized his technique. Illusion is the essential of all drama, the last survival of that religious ecstasy to which the terrified savage surrenders himself when, in the imagined security of mass emotion, he interprets an incomprehensible creation in the terms of a mechanical ritual. Drama as a form of artistic expression is only one of the few instances in which man finds compensation for his sense of insignificance in the universe, by creating in opposition a universe of his own. It is only in this way he can give meaning to a life which is otherwise swamped in the vast perspectives of cosmic time and space. The child already reacts against the gaunt objectivity of existence in its endlessly repeated games and make-believe, and the grown man continues the same process in all his activities, twiddling his thumbs and ritualistically repeating the same mental and physical movements to pass the time and distract him from the approach of death, pretending to read a meaning into life which he cannot find. Art gives to life an illusory intensification of experience and compensates the shortcomings of human existence by creating a reality in which man is no longer the victim but the master. Of all arts, drama, the great art of make-believe, is perhaps the most significant. Here it is possible for a brief interval to accept the illusion of a man-made reality, where man plays the central part and where his stature increases in pathos the more he is portrayed as the plaything of an eyeless destiny. There are two ways in which this illusion of reality can be created: either by the construction of a purely imaginary world, or by the reconstruction of the world of appearances with man as the central figure. Ibsen as a dramatist used both these methods, and obtained the greatest illusion by means of the second, whereas in his later plays he blended the two and left open chinks in his pseudo-realistic world, through which we may catch glimpses of the fantastic world beyond. In his creation of the illusion he used a series of conventions, some inherited, some stipulated by himself. It is with the examination of the conventions of his technique that the rest of this study is concerned.

CHAPTER IV

SETTINGS AND STAGE DIRECTIONS

IBSEN wrote *Catilina*, practically speaking, without any knowledge of the stage. His next play, *The Warrior's Barrow*, was also written without much acquaintance with the practical side of the theatre, but it procured him a free ticket to the performances of the Christiania Theatre which he was otherwise too poor to frequent. He there became familiar with the current repertoire, and in his criticisms we find him paying considerable attention to the style of acting and the setting of the plays. But it is also obvious from these articles that Ibsen had not as yet 'got behind the scenes'. His chance came when Ole Bull summoned him to the Bergen National Theatre in 1851. On November 6th he signed a contract to 'assist the theatre as dramatic author'. This post as salaried dramatist was rather an anomaly in a theatre of such small means, and in order to initiate Ibsen into the intricacies of the stage the management decided, in February 1852, to give him a travelling grant for the purpose of studying European stages. On April 15th Ibsen left Bergen for Copenhagen in the company of the actors Johannes and Luise Brun, who were to study dancing and acting with Danish instructors. Ibsen was to produce a report of his studies and had been promised the position of stage manager and producer in the theatre on his return.

Ibsen installed himself in a room in Reverentsgaden 205, which he saw advertised as follows: 'For a gallant gentleman a large, light, finely furnished apartment with three windows looking on to the street in a gallant house.'

He had a personal introduction from Judge Hansson in Bergen to the manager of the Royal Theatre, the philosopher-critic-poet J. L. Heiberg, and was received very kindly, though the earnest little Norwegian was not a little dumbfounded when he was invited to dinner and his elegant host dismissed all talk of the theatre, and spoke only of 'culinary matters'. He was, however, handed on to the care of the stage manager of the theatre, Thomas Overskou, who was most helpful. The season was then approaching its close: no new plays were being rehearsed and Ibsen was advised to spend the first part of his time in the auditorium watching the finished products. He was given a free pass to all performances, and this 'little hard-bitten Norwegian with his watchful eyes', as Overskou called him, had excellent opportunities to witness a very extensive repertoire. He saw Phister play in Holberg, N. P. Nielsen in Oehlenschlæger, he saw for the first time Michael Wiehe, whose performances he recalled many years afterwards, and, most important of all, he saw Høedt play his realistic version of Hamlet in direct opposition to the idealistic manner which was favoured by J. L. Heiberg and the Germans. He saw Shakespeare's *Lear, Romeo and Juliet* and *As You Like It*, saw plays by Scribe and admired their stage structure; and also plays by Hertz, Hostrup and Heiberg. Besides the Royal Theatre there were two theatres in Copenhagen at the time, the Casino and the Royal Court Theatre, both of which he visited. The latter Ibsen attended for a gala performance at which Hostrup's play, *Master and Apprentice*, was produced for the first time. This work probably influenced Ibsen's future production in its attack on the morals of journalism, while Hostrup's use of supernatural creatures may have played its part in the forming of the fantastic play Ibsen was writing at the time, his *Midsummer Eve*.

When the season was over Overskou at last took Ibsen behind the scenes at the Royal Theatre. Of Ibsen's impressions we can only judge from a letter he wrote a few days before (May 30th, 1852): 'The theatre's season ended last Friday', he writes. 'Mr. Overskou has promised to make me acquainted with the theatre machinery, etc., which was impossible during the season; however the machinery at the Copenhagen theatre is not of the best, and I hope in this respect that the German theatres will make a much more profitable study.'[1] Ibsen remained in Copenhagen another

[1] During Ibsen's visit in Copenhagen the Royal Theatre possessed very primitive stage apparatus. The auditorium and the stage were illuminated with oil lamps of the Argant round burner type. The scenery was changed by shifting the flats into the wings and the back drop was rolled or folded. Not until 1855 was the theatre rebuilt, and now it acquired the characteristic fly gallery or equivalent of the modern gridiron, which made it possible to change scenes by lifting up bodily all back-cloths and sets into the space over the stage. Gas-pipes were laid throughout the theatre for the introduction of gas lighting when the projected town supply should be available. Characteristic of the conservatism of the theatre was the opposition of the actors to the introduction of gas into the green-rooms. This was due to the fact that each actor was given a ration of candles, which he saved for home use. When gas threatened to do away with this useful perquisite they all unanimously declared that it was impossible to make up except by candlelight.

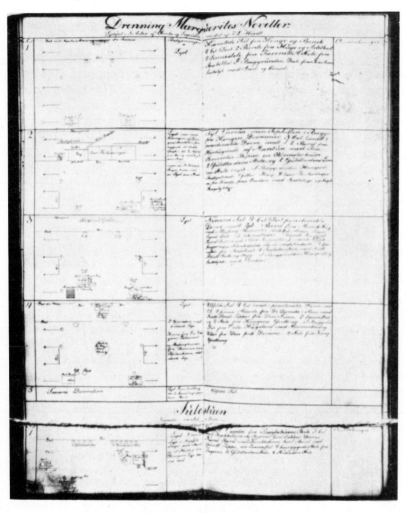

Page from the Stage Manager's book at Copenhagen
Royal Theatre, early 1850s
(Scribe's *Les Contes de la Reine de Navarre* and Holberg's *Julestuen*)

Page from the Stage Manager's book at the Bergen National Theatre, 1853 week studying the stage and procuring copies of plays, a costume book and musical scores for the Bergen theatre. His choice of repertoire in Bergen was profoundly influenced by his stay in Copenhagen, in his productions of Scribe and of Scribe's Danish imitators, a repertoire well suited to the public with which he had to reckon at home.

Ibsen left Copenhagen on June 6th and arrived in Dresden on the 9th, where he stayed with a veterinary surgeon Tröitzk, at Töpfergasse 13. He had letters of introduction to the Norwegian painter and art professor, J. C. Dahl, but on account of the latter's absence on holiday had to wait till the 16th before he met him. On June 24th he wrote: 'He [Dahl] has now managed to procure me access behind the scenes at the theatre, which I am certain will be of great value to me, since everything is in excellent condition.'[1] He had to pay for his admission to the performances, but in spite of straitened circumstances managed to see some sterling productions. He saw the Pole, Bogumil Dawison, play Hamlet, and he also saw Emil Devrient. Of other Shakespearean plays here he saw *A Midsummer Night's Dream* and *Richard III.* Hettner's book *Das moderne Drama* had just come out, and here he was once more able to find support for his admiration of Scribe and Shakespeare. Hettner's book he had probably already read in Copenhagen, as the paper *Faedrelandet* advertised the opening of a new newspaper reading-room in Silkegade where Hettner's *Das moderne Drama* and his *Die romantische Schule* were displayed for the benefit of the readers.

In September Ibsen returned to Bergen. Here he took up his new post as stage manager and producer. He was not independent as he had hoped, but under the control of Hermann Laading, who was also given the same title, a situation which annoyed Ibsen and even resulted in making him challenge his superior to a duel. Whatever his official position may have been, Ibsen nevertheless both wrote and produced plays on his own. He was now able to put into practice the results of his studies abroad. His producer's note-book from the years 1852-1854 is preserved in the Bergen Museum, and this not only gives a very good idea of how he set

---

[1] The Dresden Hoftheater had been rebuilt in 1840, twelve years before Ibsen's visit, under the direction of Professor Semper and von Wolframdorf. It accommodated more than 1800 spectators and was a model of modernity with regard to scenery and stage equipment.

to work but is also instructive in throwing light on his own dramatic technique.

For the period 1852-1853 his method of preparation was as follows. In a broad column on the left side of the page he drew a painstaking diagram of the stage setting. In every case we find him using flats set behind one another, whether for indoor or outdoor scenery. These were of course painted in perspective to give an illusion of reality. The theatre museum at Bergen has some amusing relics from this period which show with what skill the scene painters could use their two dimensions. The diagrams were then filled in with the positions of the characters, whose movements were indicated by dotted lines. To the right of this diagram was a smaller column for cues, and to the right of this again a broad column with notes indicating the movements and gestures of the characters. Pages without diagrams contained four columns, two for cues and two for notes on the movements of the actors. In 1853 the arrangement of his notes takes another form, more detailed and more practical for reference. Each page has four different columns, one for stage directions, one for positions, one for properties and a fourth for notes. The column of stage directions is filled in either with written descriptions of the setting or diagrams, the latter often in two planes, vertical and horizontal, and frequently executed in colour. The stage directions are divided into scenes according to exits and entrances in the French tradition, a convention which Ibsen used with his own plays at the time and only gave up when he wrote *Love's Comedy* in 1862. The directions are written and the diagrams are drawn with 'right' and 'left' as seen from the stage, in direct contradiction to his later custom and in conformity with the French models which he so closely followed in his own earlier plays. In a letter to August Lindberg (November 22nd, 1884) he wrote: 'In reply to your question I hasten to inform you that *The Wild Duck*, like all my plays, is set from the auditorium and not from the stage. I set everything as I see it before me when writing.' When Ibsen made this change, it is impossible to say with any certainty, but it would seem to date from *The League of Youth*, which was written with the conscious intent to create a realistic illusion, or from *Ghosts*, where Ibsen declared his intention to be 'to give the reader the impression that he was experiencing a piece of reality while reading'. It is at any rate connected with the intention to write for the reader and not for the producer, an intention which is not obvious with Ibsen until he has left Norway and has severed his connection with the stage.

This producer's note-book, together with the plays Ibsen wrote on his return to Norway, show clearly what he learnt from his study tour. He had grasped the importance of the visual stage effect. Not only can we follow this in the diagrams and notes of his producer's book, but also in the wealth of stage directions which now fill his plays. The contrast between *Catilina* and *Midsummer Eve*, the play he wrote during his tour, is very striking in this respect. The first act of *Catilina* is headed: 'On the Flaminian highway outside Rome. A wooded slope. In the background rise the heights and walls of the town. It is evening.' The setting of the first act of *Midsummer Eve* is described as follows: 'Mrs. Berg's garden, which is cut off from the highroad in the background by a fence with a gate. On the right the main building, erected in an attractive modern style; on the left further up stage an old-fashioned timbered house.' The stage directions in *Catilina* give only a hint of the locality, they give no indication of the distribution of the various sets about the stage. There could, however, be no doubt about the stage plan in *Midsummer Eve*. The setting here is bounded by foreground, background and the right and left wings, which is not the case in *Catilina*. Ibsen has begun to set his plays in relation to a definite stage. The stage directions in *Catilina* and *The Warrior's Barrow*, with their signboard curtness, are an inheritance from Shakespeare's editors, handed down via Schiller and Oehlenschlæger. The extensive stage directions which we meet for the first time with Ibsen in *Midsummer Eve* are taken direct from contemporary French intrigue drama, which in this respect as in many others was a direct offshoot of the realistic English *bourgeois* drama of the eighteenth century.

The lavish settings and numerous changes of scene in Ibsen's Bergen plays would lead one to believe that the Bergen stage possessed extensive technical resources. This was by no means the case. The theatre was built in 1800 in neo-classic style with a stage which was singularly ill equipped. In 1825 a Danish portrait painter was engaged to furnish the stage with modern machinery. This consisted in a variation of the apparatus which was employed in the eighteenth-century court theatres, and as far as scene shifting was concerned it was very efficient. The flats in the wings were mounted in grooves and connected to a central winch below the stage. Each flat had a group of two, three or four grooves in which the successive sets could be mounted simultaneously. The winch could then in a very short time pull into position or withdraw any one of the sets. The scts worked in combination with a back-cloth which was quickly changed by folding or rolling. This expeditious method of scene-shifting together with the scene-painter's proficiency in perspective painting made practically speaking any scene possible. Ibsen's later demands for realism discarded two-dimensional perspective scenery and introduced three-dimensional scenery with walls and solid properties. The wagon or lift stage had by then not been invented, no one yet thought of using curtains, and it took much more time to change scenes of this kind. This latter consideration no doubt contributed to Ibsen's artistic economy in the unity of place which dominates in his early realistic plays.

Lighting was always of supreme importance to Ibsen in creating the atmosphere of a setting. In a letter to Schrøder with reference to the setting of *The Wild Duck*, he wrote: 'The lighting also has its significance; it is different for each act and is intended to correpond to the mood which gives each of the acts its special character.' This symbolical use of light is characteristic of Ibsen even in his earliest works. In his preface to the second edition of his first work, *Catilina*, he dwells on the fact that the play was written at night and adds: 'I believe that this is the unconscious reason for nearly all the action taking place at night.' The play was undoubtedly written with a sense of the importance of the lighting in order to give it atmosphere, but certainly without regard for the technical possibilities. Not until Ibsen came to Dresden did he realize the possibilities of the lighting effects embodied in gas illumination.[1] Oil lamps were used in Bergen until 1856 when gas was introduced in the theatre. His appreciation of the importance of being able to control the strength of the lighting with gas

[1] Gas was first used for stage lighting when the German F. A. Wintzler installed gas lighting in the Lyceum Theatre, London, in 1806. Gas was common in London theatres much earlier than on the Continent, where the Argant oil lamp was in use until the 1850s. With the latter the lights were controlled in the same ingenious manner as in the days of candles. The lamps were shaded with coloured glass, taffeta or gauze, the footlights could be darkened or hidden entirely by sinking them in a trough and the lights in the wings were regulated by cowls.

illumination can be seen in *Midsummer Eve*, the play which he wrote abroad under the influence of his impressions there. The first act begins in the evening and a stage direction tells us that it 'begins to get dark'. In the second act 'it is night; the moon is in the sky'. The scene is then suddenly lit up by the opening of the fairy mound, a purely operatic stage effect, and the third act shows us the whole stage in bright daylight again. The play was a failure, and this no doubt was largely due to the fact that the theatre machinery and lighting was not equal to Ibsen's demands. Anyhow it is noticeable how Ibsen's next play, *Lady Inger*, follows the model of *Catilina* and passes in a crescendo of gloom, completely abandoning the effects of light contrasts which he developed to such an art later, and only indulging in such effects as would conform to the demands of realism on a lamp-lit stage. Ibsen, in his dual position of dramatist and stage manager, would naturally advocate such a reform as the introduction of gas into the theatre, and it appears not unlikely that he was responsible for its installation. Gas illumination was used in Bergen for the first time in 1856, and the theatre was one of the first buildings to take advantage of it. *The Feast at Solhaug*, which was produced in January 1856, shows as yet no signs of the effect of the new illumination, but the next play, *Olaf Liljekrans*, is full of lighting effects, dusk, dawn and a midnight fire. The next play, *The Warriors of Helgeland*, with its full-blooded realism of setting, spares no opportunity for stage effect, and it is significant that Ibsen first sent his play to the Christiania Theatre before producing it at his own, because he knew among other things that it possessed a very much better technical equipment. From now on Ibsen's stage directions never omit indications of lighting. Here in the first act the curtain rises on 'winter, thick snowy weather and storm'. This is followed later by the stage direction: 'The storm has ceased during the previous scene; the midday sun appears like a red disk on the horizon.' The second act is by contrast illuminated by a log fire, the third is daylight, and the fourth act is lit by torches and the rising moon, which spreads an atmosphere of peace after the passing storm. Light is from now onwards used by Ibsen not only to indicate the passage of time, but also as a symbolical accompaniment to the action. His early appreciation of the importance and possibility of light effects on the stage he owed to his visit to Dresden in 1852.

During his tour in Denmark and Germany Ibsen became acquainted with contemporary stage machinery and lighting, together with the routine of producing. We have seen the fruit of his experiences in the detailed settings and stage directions of the plays he wrote at the time, which form a parallel to the painstaking plans in his producer's note-book. So far we have watched him exploiting the technical resources with which he became acquainted. If we now turn to the individualization of Ibsen's technique of setting and stage directions, we find here, as everywhere, a growing tendency towards realistic illusion combined with an equally strong inclination to romantic symbolism. It is the latter which dominates in the later plays.

In *Catilina* and *The Warrior's Barrow* there is no conscious attempt at realistic setting. *The Ptarmigan of Justedal* and *Midsummer Eve* offer only vague indications of conventional sets and properties. The disposition of the various scenes is indicated, but not the nature of the individual objects. In the former we meet with a 'wild but beautiful part of Justedalen', which only evokes a very vague picture. In the latter we know that the main building is 'erected in an attractive modern style' while the building on the left is an 'old-fashioned timbered house'. This tells us nothing of the peculiarities of the two buildings, but is rather an indication for the property-man as to what sets are to be used. In *Lady Inger* and *The Feast at Solhaug* we find a slight increase in detail, but we are dealing with standard props all the time, 'a magnificent room', 'an old-fashioned carved high seat', and so forth. The same is the case with *Olaf Liljekrans*. *The Warriors of Helgeland* is the first play with a specifically realistic setting and it is significant that it was written in the year that Ibsen left Bergen and no longer had to reckon with the theatre stock of properties and sets. The setting of the first scene is as follows: 'A high shore which slopes steeply down to the sea in the background. On the left a boat-house, on the right mountains and pine woods. The masts of two warships can be seen down in the bay; far away on the right rocks and high islands; the sea is very rough, it is winter with thick snowy weather and storm.' The striking feature about this setting is not so much the absence of standard props and scenery but the way in which Ibsen sets an outdoor scene and overcomes false perspective. He uses a high foreground which masks receding perspective, behind which the back-cloth can represent the middle and far distance without risk of showing up the actors out of proportion. The foreground is the only area of the stage on which the actors appear and their size is then always in proper relation to the scenery. This method of giving an illusion of reality to outdoor settings was in future always employed by Ibsen in only two variations. The first was the high foreground which we meet again in *The Lady from the Sea, John Gabriel Borkman* and *When We Dead Awaken*, the second the fenced-in garden where the fence has the function of masking the perspective, a setting which we remember as far back as *Midsummer Eve* and which recurs in *The Lady from the Sea, Little Eyolf* and *When We Dead Awaken*.

One frequently hears of the stuffy atmosphere of Ibsen's plays, the atmosphere which pervades the indoor settings of his modern tragedies. From 1877, when the *Pillars of Society* was published, until 1886, the date of the publication of *Rosmersholm*, all his plays were set indoors, while the first three of these six take place in one and the same room. After this date there is only one totally indoor play, *Hedda Gabler*; two are set entirely out of doors (*The Lady from the Sea, When We Dead Awaken*) and the remaining three have both outdoor and indoor settings. The indoor setting is the direct result of Ibsen's conscious effort to create a realistic illusion, while its abandonment coincides with his reversion to romantic symbolism. Even more than in the case of the outdoor setting, the interior had to overcome the difficulties of perspective. As we can see from Ibsen's diagrams for interior settings, the Bergen theatre used the type of scenery which was common at the time; that is to say that the side walls of a room were represented by transverse flies set parallel behind one another as in the outdoor scenes, while the back wall was represented by a flapping back-cloth with doors and windows. The whole pro-scenium opening was used for rooms of all dimensions and the illusion of varying size was brought about by the false perspective of the scene-painter. In the setting of Ibsen's *Lady Inger*, for instance, the room in the first act would occupy as much stage space as the knight's hall in the third, though the latter might of course use a little deeper stage. In the impoverished theatre at Bergen economy was everything as regards properties and scenery, and the painter was in consequence called upon to include in his settings flat pasteboard cupboards, chairs and ornaments which the theatre could not afford to procure in the solid. The effect of these settings as a peep-show panorama was often very illusory, but the impression was immediately destroyed by the movements of the actors. A reaction against this type of indoor setting began to make itself felt in Europe about this time. The study of the Elizabethan stage, which had begun with Tieck, led to various attempts at reconstruction, especially in the use of the little inner stage and the curtain background. Laube, in his historical productions, had already begun to simplify this scenery and had set his actors against a plain background, but the tendency of the day was for historical realism and against stylization, and here it was that the Meiningen Company seemed to have impressed Ibsen with their solid realistic scenery. Solid interior walls and ceilings for modern settings had already been introduced previously in France and England, and it may well be that Ibsen during his residence in Germany had seen imitations of this in modern plays.[1] The settings of *Emperor and Galilean* are mostly outdoor ones and the few interiors show as yet no signs of modern realism. But when we come to *Pillars of Society* it is a different matter. The earliest notes for this play date from 1870 and it was not finished until 1877, the year after Ibsen saw the first Meininger performances. As far as we can judge from the notes and sketches before 1876 the scene was changed in each act. The first act took place in Consul Bernick's morning-room, the second in the garden, the third on a road by the shore and the fourth in a wood. After 1876 the setting immediately took shape and was restricted to Consul Bernick's morning-room for all the acts, while the directions give the most detailed description of the stage hitherto provided by Ibsen. In this setting he has transferred the historical

---

[1] The use of enclosed rooms with ceilings and walls instead of open wings is cited in the *Allgemeines Theaterlexikon* of 1846 as already being characteristic of the English stage. Here also is mentioned the device of altering the depth of the stage and the size of the proscenium opening in order to approach more realistically the dimensions of the interiors, in contrast to outdoor scenery. Likewise the Théâtre du Gymnase in Paris adopted a manner of realistic staging, and the conventional three doors in the back-cloth, punctuated with architecturally impossible windows, were abandoned. As far as ceilings are concerned it is interesting to recall that the Italian renaissance theatre was in the habit of using a sky or cloud roof to the stage for outside settings (something like the sky-cyclorama), which was only replaced by flies and an open roof when flying-machines were introduced. Also the use of solid scenery and doors that can be banged is only a reversion to the permanent stage structures of such theatres as the Teatro Olympico at Vicenza, which in its own turn is only Palladio's attempt to reconstruct a Roman theatre.

realism of the Meininger into modern surroundings, and has combined the interior with the fenced-in garden exterior to give a complete illusion of the 'fourth wall'. We have only to compare this scene with a corresponding scene in *The League of Youth*, its predecessor as a modern play, to see how Ibsen had individualized his technique. The second act of the latter play has the following setting: 'The chamberlain's morning-room. Elegant furniture, a piano, flowers and rare plants. Entrance door in the background. On the left a door into the dining-room; on the right several glass doors opening into the garden.' In this case we are still dealing with props and standard sets. In the *Pillars of Society* we find the following setting: 'A spacious morning-room in Consul Bernick's house. In the foreground on the left there is a door leading into the consul's room; further back on the same wall is a similar door. In the middle of the opposite wall is a fairly large entrance-door. The wall in the background is almost entirely composed of mirrors, with an open door leading out on to broad garden steps, over which is stretched an awning. At the bottom of the steps one can see part of the garden, which is enclosed by a fence with a little gate. On the other side of the fence, and parallel to it, runs a street which is flanked on the opposite side by small brightly-painted wooden houses. It is summer and the sun is shining warmly. People pass by in the street from time to time; they stop and converse; they go and make purchases in a shop on the corner, etc. . . .' Here there is no question of standard props or sets, the whole scene is an individual solid structure. We find Ibsen for the first time giving directions for a realistic setting and following the example of contemporary producers. The producers had hitherto looked to the past for their dramatists and now Ibsen appeared and immediately carried them off their feet.

With *Pillars of Society*, Ibsen inaugurates his series of modern indoor plays, and he becomes a master in electrifying these settings with dramatic potentiality. The dramatic importance of the ground plan and elevation of the houses in which his plays are set, together very often with the locality in which the houses stand, is very great in Ibsen's work. He transforms and adapts to his own use the secret stairs and trap-doors and sliding panels of romantic melodrama, so that his doors and curtains and windows are equally pregnant with secrets in spite of their prosaic surroundings. Ibsen once spoke of himself as a builder, and there is no doubt that he had a supreme sense of the dramatic in architecture. We remember houses and parts of houses from Ibsen's plays as well as we know our own. His insistence on architecture begins with *A Doll's House*. The room in this case has four doors, each of them having their function, while two of them, the door to Helmer's study and the one into the hall, become the focus of dramatic tension, especially when Krogstad's letter is lying in the hall letter-box. In the course of the action we learn that the flat is on the first floor, we know where the kitchen and the nursery and Nora's bedroom are, and we hear the music from the fancy-dress party in the flat above. The effect of this technique is to give one a sense of tremendous dramatic activity focused on the one room visible on the stage, and also to give this one room an extension far beyond its real dimensions. This latter effect is increased by noises off and talking off the stage. In *John Gabriel Borkman* a similar illusion of architectural solidity is brought about by the continuity of the four acts in which the action progresses without any time interval. At the end of the first act in Mrs. Borkman's room on the ground floor we hear music from Borkman's room above. The second act opens in Borkman's room where Frida Foldal is playing the piano; in the third Borkman comes downstairs and at the end rushes out of the hall door into the snow. The fourth act shows the outside of the house and Borkman walking out. The door to Borkman's room is also charged with dramatic tension. He is always waiting for the knock which will announce the arrival of the delegation which is to clear his reputation. A similar dramatic door we have in *The Master Builder* when Solness says, 'One of these days youth will come here knocking at the door', in response to which Hilde Wangel seals his fate by her prompt knocking. In *Rosmersholm* we find a genuine survival of romantic melodrama in the curtain behind which Rebekka overhears Rosmer's conversation with Mortensgård.

Ibsen's appreciation of the dramatic value of a realistic setting is well illustrated in the case of *The Wild Duck*. In this case a study of the drafts of the play shows exactly with what care he worked out the details. The last four acts of the play pass in Hjalmar Ekdal's studio, and in the back wall we see the door which leads into the weird garret where the duck and the rabbits and pigeons are kept. In the second draft the stage directions describe the door as follows: 'A large double door in the middle of the back wall constructed so that it can be pushed aside.' When Ekdal insists on showing Gregers the attic the directions state: 'Ekdal and Hjalmar have gone to the back wall and each push aside the upper part of their half of the door.' In the third act the same process is repeated: 'Hjalmar and Ekdal open the upper part of the half-doors to the garret.' Ekdal squeezes himself into the garret by opening the lower half of the doors slightly. Then Hjalmar 'pulls a string; a piece of stretched fishing-net slides down in front of the door opening'. In the play the door into the garret is constructed differently. Instead of being divided into four parts, which enables the upper half to be open while the lower remains shut, it is made of only two partitions, one on each side which open and disclose the whole floor of the garret. It is a 'broad double sliding door'. In the second act Hjalmar and Ekdal disclose the whole attic in the moonlight, the animals being hidden in the shadow, whereas formerly the floor was not visible. In the third act Hjalmar and Ekdal again open each of the sliding doors and disclose the whole attic in the sunshine, together with its inhabitants. After this full glimpse Hjalmar 'pulls a string; from inside a curtain is lowered, the bottom part of which consists of a strip of old sailcloth, the upper of a piece of stretched fishing net. Thus the floor of the garret is no longer visible'. In the earlier version the contents of the garret were seen by the actors alone and the duck still remained a formless figure for the audience. In the play the garret is fully revealed to the spectators with its bizarre display of animals and rubbish. The momentary glimpse of what is behind gives the sailcloth and the closed door a weird suggestive power which was absent when the duck remained unseen and unreal. This is only one instance of Ibsen's capacity for increasing the dramatic effect by a pure arrangement of scenery.

This constructive sense in Ibsen's indoor settings is equally strong in all his later plays and it is combined with great economy of material. His stages were set with regard to the function of the various units, the doors, windows and pieces of furniture, and he cleared the stage of all the superfluous junk that was popular in the dazzling settings of French social dramas. His settings were inspired with a sympathy for the effect of *milieu* on the characters and often possess a dramatic quality independent of the characters

71

themselves.[1] Concentration and elimination were his principles in developing dialogue and character, and it was the same principles he applied to realistic settings; his dramatic sense was greatly aided by his painter's eye in their conception and they form one of the characteristic features of Ibsen's drama.

With all this outward realism Ibsen's settings are basically only symbolical comments on the action of his plays, and this is especially true in the case of his outdoor settings, where his nature lacks freshness and has the character of a mere accessory to human emotions. This undertone of romantic symbolism pervades all Ibsen's plays even during his most realistic period. In the one case his settings and stage effects take the form of a symbolical accompaniment to the action. Reference has already been made to the symbolical nature of the lighting in Ibsen's plays and to the instructions which were sent to his producer Schrøder with regard to one of his most realistic plays, *The Wild Duck*. Other effects also play a similar part in creating mood and atmosphere. In his first play *Catilina*, at the moment when the hero decides to knife his wife Aurelia and utters the fateful words

[1] The creation of *milieu* by stage setting was a product of eighteenth-century *bourgeois* drama. The *milieu* in Shakespeare's plays is created by the dialogue and not by the setting or the stage directions. In the first scene of *Hamlet* we know that it is twelve o'clock on a cold silent night without the aid of any stage directions beyond those indicating the locality, and even these are superfluous. Ibsen on the other hand relies very much on staging and this is occasionally supplemented by the mime, ballet or tableau to accentuate the atmosphere. Hjalmar Ekdal is silently admired by his family as he plays the flute and the scene is a brilliant travesty of the sentimental *genre* pictures of the *comédie larmoyante*. Nora playing with her children is another example. When the atmosphere in *A Doll's House* becomes too tense for expression in words, Nora dances her wild tarantella. Another device is crowd effects to evoke an atmosphere, but Ibsen seldom uses crowd scenes like Shakespeare. He fails to conjure up a sense of *milieu* by the crowd scenes in *Emperor and Galilean*, though his manipulation of crowds and large numbers on the stage is very skilful in plays like *The League of Youth, The Enemy of the People, Pillars of Society* and in the scene with all the guests in *The Wild Duck*. He is unlike his contemporaries, the naturalistic authors, who loved creating *milieu* by such effects as real meals on the stage. The breakfast in *The Wild Duck* is the only instance of this in his work. Such an accessory as money does however play a large part in evoking a realistic atmosphere in his plays, especially in its relation to the individual's struggle for existence and work, in contrast to Augier with whom it had an ideal value and chiefly took the form of presents, dowries or inheritances. Money, for instance, stamps the two *milieux* of *The Wild Duck*, the rich Werle household and the Ekdal family who complain of the exorbitant price of butter. In the later plays however money loses its realistic value, Ibsen the affluent capitalist no longer remembers the poverty of his youth, and with the financier *John Gabriel Borkman* it assumes all the magic potentialities of romantic gold.

'She shall die', they are accompanied by 'a flash of lightning and a clap of thunder' in true melodramatic style. This type of stage effect is very frequent in all Ibsen's plays, and is a genuine survival of the romantic conception of nature as an operatic setting for human emotions. *Ghosts* is set against the background of a 'fjord landscape veiled in steady rain', and the ghastly final scene is played in ironical contrast on a fine morning, when the rain has stopped, in the rays of the rising sun. Ibsen never freed himself from the romantic convention of ending a tragedy with a symbolically harmonious sunrise; very different from Strindberg who sent the manuscript of his play *Creditors* to Bonnier with the comment that it was 'even better than *Lady Julia* with three characters, a table and two chairs, and without a sunrise'. The atmosphere of boredom and social degeneracy in *Hedda Gabler* is enhanced by the autumn tints and falling leaves, and the fatal avalanche at the close of *When We Dead Awaken* is a complete parallel to the similar catastrophe at the end of *Brand*, with all its poetic symbolism. Ibsen's nature, for all its realistic appurtenances, is reducible in fact to two categories. The first offers a setting for all Ibsen's ideals of freedom, individuality and truth, the scenes in which light predominates and which take place on mountain heights or open spaces; the second acts as a setting for the vices which Ibsen castigates, in which the illumination is subdued and the atmosphere stuffy, the gloomy interiors which are contrasted with the wide open spaces of land and water outside. Allmers returns from the freedom of the hills to his depressing home; Rebekka West, who loves the sea and the wild coast of Finmarken, is caged in at Rosmersholm; and Rubek leaves the lowlands and human habitations behind him to begin life again with Irene on the mountain tops.

Another type of symbolical setting with Ibsen is the one that brings about its effect by parallels or contrasts. From Scandinavian romanticism, particularly from Oehlenschlæger and Tegnér, Ibsen inherits one type of antithetical setting, the contrast of paganism and christianity. We meet this for the first time in his early work *The Warrior's Barrow*, and it pervades everywhere in the realistic settings of *Emperor and Galilean*. The opening scene of the play strikes immediately the note of dramatic conflict. 'Easter night in Constantinople. The stage represents an open space with trees, bushes and overturned statues in the neighbour-

hood of the imperial palace. In the background is the Court
Church, splendidly illuminated.' The contrast of the illuminated
church and the overturned idols gives the keynote to the play.
This use of contrast in settings recurs very frequently for the
illumination of other themes. The conflict of truth and falsehood
in *Pillars of Society* is brought home by the contrast of the stuffy
morning-room with the sunny day outside, and the crisis is precipi-
tated when Lona Hessel enters and draws aside the curtains,
opens the windows and the big french window in the background
with the words: 'We must have the place aired.' A similar
contrast is met in the flowers and family portraits of *Rosmersholm*. Together with the contrast setting we also find Ibsen
making use of parallels, as for instance the last four acts of *The
Wild Duck*, which gain much of their effect by the juxtaposition
of the Ekdals' home and the lumber-room with all its weird
inhabitants and rubbish.

Closely connected with the above-mentioned forms of symbolical setting is Ibsen's frequent use of symbolical tableaux, in
preference always at the end of the play. This is an old dramatic
device, very frequent in the sentimental drama of the eighteenth
century, a device adopted by Lessing and Schiller and practised
in excess by nineteenth-century French dramatists. Its symbolical
effect was thought to enhance the harmony of the happy ending,
but Ibsen even uses it long after accepting the tragic ending as the
only one possible, in order to alleviate the harshness of the
catastrophe. Like Hebbel, who in theory opposed the harmonious endings of the German classical school, Ibsen still
retained a belief in the triumph of the idea or the redemption of
the individual's soul. The triumph of woman's love is epitomized
in the end of Ibsen's first play where Catilina and Aurelia die in
one another's arms in the rays of the rising sun, a tableau which
has its exact parallel in the terrible concluding scene of one of
Ibsen's most realistic plays, *Ghosts*. This tendency pervades all
Ibsen's plays, whether the *milieu* is historical, imaginary or
modern, whether the plays are comedies or tragedies. *The Pretenders* ends with Håkon symbolically stepping over Skule's
corpse, *Pillars of Society* with an ostentatious conversion and
shaking of hands, and *John Gabriel Borkman* finishes on a note of
rather artificial pathos when the two sisters stand hand in hand in
reconciliation over Borkman's dead body. But Ibsen does not

necessarily restrict his tableaux to the ends of his plays. His *tableau* scenery is often arranged so as to enable the characters to group themselves in an effective manner. The most outstanding instance of this is in the second act of *When We Dead Awaken*, when Irene and Rubek take up positions on the stage which exactly correspond to the grouping of the figures in 'The Day of Resurrection', the piece of statuary which Rubek is describing. This preference for tableaux is the expression of a romantic sense of composition which he developed as a painter and learnt to appreciate in Italy. From Rome he wrote to Brandes and expressed his admiration for baroque and Gothic architecture, for Michael Angelo and Roman sculpture as opposed to Hellenistic, because of the dramatic and individualistic qualities they possessed. There is something of the baroque and Gothic sense of force and involved design in all Ibsen's work, not least in the recurrence of tableaux, and this again forms another link between Ibsen and the romantic revival which left such an indelible mark on his technique.

The stage directions which will be considered here are those which apply to the appearance, costume, gestures and diction of the actors, not those concerned in any way with the setting.

In early drama the stage directions were not printed, or were restricted to marking the entrances and exits of the protagonists. They remained as rubrics in the producers' books, a very good example of which we find in the le Mans mysteries published by Gustave Cohen. Shakespeare's stage directions in the early quartos and folios were extended to indications of place and gesture, but they are almost certainly interpolations of the publishers. In Jacobean drama stage directions were extended, and in England and France they became a necessary part of comedies when the plays were printed for reading. Scapin, without stage directions about the sack in which he hides, would be unintelligible to the reader. Stage directions became more and more necessary for the understanding of situations and miming in comedy, though they still remained sparse in tragedy. After the eighteenth-century *mélange des genres*, however, they became common in serious drama, and the demands of realism, together with the serious competition of the novel, forced the directions to become more extensive and to include not only indications of exits and entrances and place, but also descriptions of gesture, expression, action, appearance and diction. Whereas Shakespeare creates a complete unity of dramatic effect by giving all his necessary indications in the dialogue, drama now began to suffer from a dualism of dialogue and stage direction. Never would it have been possible for Shakespeare to use the dualistic method of characterization employed by Schiller, one of whose characters protests, 'I am not trembling' and is immediately shown up by the stage direction 'trembles violently'. This dualism and descriptiveness of direction was preserved in nineteenth-century intrigue drama and was adopted by Ibsen. His progress towards a realistic technique is marked by an elimination of this dualism, while he exaggerated the descriptive nature of the stage directions.

Ibsen's first play *Catilina* shows how he adopted the rudiments of dualistic stage directions. The text here seldom speaks for the characters without the author's comment; they speak 'aside' or 'whispering' or 'talking to themselves'; the degrees and nature of their emotions are registered by indications such as 'cheerfully', 'anxiously', 'violently', 'beseechingly', and the voice register is recorded on a scale ranging between 'quietly' and 'loudly'. As far as the movements, gestures and facial expressions of the characters are concerned, they also are indicated with precision and are qualified with adjectives of approbation or disapproval. Catilina 'comes down on to the road', 'points towards the town and says', Manlius 'enters in an impetuous mood', Furia 'speaks with a savage smile'. Ibsen, however, never went so far as to describe the costume or the appearance of the characters until 1857 when he wrote *The Warriors of Helgeland*, his first consciously realistic play. After his study tour abroad his use of stage directions is increased and his plays are loaded with them. They are particularly necessary if one is to follow the complicated intrigues, such as the poisoned cup which changes hands so often in *The Feast at Solhaug* or the fate of the letters and documents in *Lady Inger*.

With *The Warriors of Helgeland* we meet a totally new technique. Ibsen here for the first time introduces a realistic description of the costume and appearance of the characters. Sigurd is 'dressed in a white tunic with a silver belt, a blue cloak, leggings, fur shoes and a steel helmet, he carries a short sword at his side'. Each character as he or she appears is described with similar exactitude. Their height and build and facial appearance are often included.

Arnulf for instance is 'tall and of gigantic build, with a long white beard, old and a little bent'. Side by side with this descriptive realism we find Ibsen abolishing much of his artificial dualism. This play is the first in which he for good and all abolished the 'aside' from the stage directions.

But Ibsen's development towards realism was not continuous. He abandoned the descriptive stage direction and retained only what was necessary to guide the actors in their movements and diction. Until 1888 we meet with very few descriptions of characters, the only memorable one being old Ekdal in *The Wild Duck*, with his threadbare jacket and high collar, his cotton gloves, his stick, his leather cap, his reddish brown, dirty wig and his little grey moustache. But towards the end of his life Ibsen became less of a dramatist and more of a novelist, and with this tendency we meet with a sudden reintroduction of the description of costume and appearance. This tendency began with general indications for costume and make-up, but Ibsen's sense of significant detail soon overestimated the capacity of any stage or the attention of any audience. With *The Lady from the Sea* in 1888 these stage directions were used again to a moderate degree. With *Hedda Gabler* two years later Ibsen embarked on the field of the psychological novel. Here the exact age of each character is given, Juliane Tesman 65, Hedda 29, Tesman 33, and so forth, together with minute details of dress and appearance, such as Hedda's 'steel-blue eyes' and Thea's 'large, round, rather protruding pale blue eyes', features which no make-up could achieve. This attention to realistic detail reaches its climax in Ibsen's most undramatic play, *Little Eyolf*. In the final version Allmers is described as 'a slim well-built man between thirty-six and thirty-seven, with kind eyes, thin brown hair and beard'. The various drafts of the play show with what pains Ibsen worked out these details. In the first draft Allmers is 'a slim, fine figure with a touch of earnestness in his features, thin dark hair and beard'. In the first revision of his first act he is described as follows, with the following erasures and insertions in the manuscript.

He is a slim [first written 'fine man'] finely built man between 36-37 [corrected from 37-38], [insert 'with kind eyes'] brown, luxuriant [corrected to 'thin'] hair and [corrected from 'but without'] beard. His features are serious and thoughtful [corrected from 'reflective']. [erased 'He has sparkling eyes'.]

This affection for detail is characteristic of his late plays and his stage directions were the predecessors of the diffuse directions we meet with in Shaw, Galsworthy and Barrie, though he avoided as much as possible the artificial dualism of French intrigue drama which survived with these latter authors. While these detailed directions had the professed intention of creating an illusion of realism they are supremely romantic in their symbolical presentation of the characters.

The symbolism in Ibsen's stage directions is constant from the beginning. When the realistic descriptions of costume and feature are introduced symbolism applies to them as well. Here, as in the case of stage settings, he makes use chiefly of contrasts and parallels to aid his characterization and the progress of the action. In his early plays his villains and villainesses are inclined to walk stealthily, to snarl and sneer and flash their eyes, while the heroes and heroines walk and talk with open hearts. When the more realistic, descriptive directions are introduced this symbolism is even more marked. The meek Dagny is dressed in red and blue while the wild Hjørdis is dressed in black, Thea Elvsted has rich wavy fair hair, wide, open frightened eyes; she is frail and pretty and poorly dressed in contrast to Hedda's brown hair, her piercing eyes, her aristocratic features and smart clothes. Symbolical contrasts of this kind are repeated again and again with Ibsen, but the symbol often stands alone as a sort of label. Brand is dressed in black, Emperor Julian appears with fingers inky from writing. The instances are so many and so obvious that it is unnecessary to stress them. Parallel symbols are also found, such as the two shots in *The Wild Duck*, both of them announced by the same stage direction but each associated with ironically contrasting incidents, the one the death of a rabbit, the other the little girl's suicide. The repetition of the fatal kiss, in the fatal dining-room, with the fatal maid, accompanied by the pop of the fatal champagne cork in *Ghosts* offers us another instance of the use of parallelism. The symbolical nature of even the most realistic of Ibsen's stage directions increases in his later work and is another characteristic of the plays of this incorrigibly romantic poet.

CHAPTER V

PLOT AND ACTION

THE word 'plot' and its French equivalent 'intrigue' are a significant loan in the vocabulary of dramatic art. While both words acquired their present sense in the seventeenth-century theatre in France and Britain, they supplanted in the course of the eighteenth and nineteenth centuries all other words such as *thème*, *trame*, action, tale, which were relegated to the field of epic and narrative. It is easy to trace their popularity back to the change which took place in dramatic technique when psychology was forsaken for situation. The mechanism of what we now know as 'intrigue technique' was developed in the course of the eighteenth century as a result of the fusion of tragedy and comedy. Diderot, for instance, in his theoretical works, insisted that characters were formed by situations. Voltaire at the same time attempted to demonstrate the importance of chance in shaping the course of history, with the result that we soon meet with a complete revolution in the technique of drama. The characters no longer decide their own destiny nor act under the influence of an inexorable fate, they lose their logical consistency and become a prey to outside situations and quite fortuitous happenings. The art of the dramatist is judged by a new set of standards according to his skill in complicating and solving situations. Drama becomes from now on a sort of riddle or puzzle, and accordingly its themes become standardized and restricted to the treatment of plots or intrigues of endlessly varying nature. The only original characters produced by this type of drama are the expert intriguer and plotter and the equally expert detective, mechanical types devoid of all emotion and acting according to certain unwritten laws in this stage game of hide and seek. Eugène Scribe became the expert exponent of this technique, and his *pièce bien faite* was a model for dramatists and a standard for the dramatic critic. Francisque Sarcey[1] of *Le Temps* became the critical theorist of this type of

[1] Francisque Sarcey acted during the last half of the nineteenth century as the Aristotle of the drawing-room drama. In 1859 he became critic of the *Opinion Nationale* and from 1867 to 1899 his lengthy theatre criticisms appeared every Monday in *Le Temps*. From the observation of the stage of the day he evolved a dramatic theory which was of considerable importance in influencing contemporary

drama and his articles read like discussions of a mathematical exercise. The logical sense of the French was now applied to the development of a chain of situations out of some fortuitous occurrence or other (an accident, a mistake) and to constructing these situations round a critical scene on which the whole play turned, the so-called *scène à faire*. Sarcey engaged in lengthy discussions upon the position of this scene in the play and the nature of the scene itself, with its various elements of surprise, suspense and revelation. The writing of a play now consisted in the development of situations up to this decisive moment with the help of an arsenal of conventional scenes, situations and characters

dramatists. These theories are contained in his weekly criticisms and in his *Essai d'une esthétique de théâtre* which was published in 1876.

He analyses the practice and convention of the stage of the day and maintains that the principles of dramatic technique are conditioned by the nature of the public, the period and the tradition. He insists on the necessity of conventions as the basis of dramatic illusion and explains this as being due to the dramatist's appeal to the mass psyche, which apprehends less subtly than the individual. He classifies the various types of drama according to the conventions which govern them.

He insisted on action as the most essential feature of drama and objected to the naturalistic and impressionistic *tranches de la vie* in which nothing happened. Action demands movement, it must have a beginning, middle and end and it ought to turn about one salient point. By movement Sarcey means the dramatist's ability to carry the spectator with him and he praises de Musset and Marivaux for their merits in this respect.

He demanded unity of impression and attacked the mixture of comic and tragic on the stage, because he insisted that the illusion was broken and the dramatist was unable to control the transition from tears to laughter with an audience of 1200 spectators. He asserts that every play ought to be constructed about a *scène à faire*, a scene in which the whole action culminated and in which the protagonists finally confronted one another. For the attainment of the maximum dramatic effect in these scenes he stressed the importance of the exposition, *l'art des préparations*, which by the devices of suspense, surprise and postponed revelation whetted the appetite of the audience for the central scene, which in a five act play ought to be placed in the fourth act. The action must develop logically and not be subject to the whims of chance, and the entries, exits and episodes must be effectively motivated.

Ibsen's estrangement from this type of drama is well demonstrated by Sarcey's own aversion to Ibsen's work. He execrated Ibsen and held up Scribe as a paragon, and he was quite unable to comprehend *Peer Gynt*, *Pillars of Society*, *A Doll's House*, *Ghosts*, *The Wild Duck*, *The Lady from the Sea* and *John Gabriel Borkman*. He always complained of lack of clarity and incomprehensible motivation. The great fault of *The Wild Duck* he considered to be Ibsen's failure to reveal the secret of the duck itself which remains a mystery to the end. His greatest stumbling-block was however Ibsen's method of retrospective exposition and he complains that '*Ibsen n'explique jamais ses pièces qu'au dernier acte, quand il les explique. Il paraît que c'est l'usage en Norvège; nous autres qui sommes des fils de la race latine, nous préférons qu'on nous mette d'abord au courant...*' Nothing however perhaps influenced the technique of Ibsen's successors so much as just this very feature which Sarcey had such difficulty in understanding.

and the legitimate use of any chance happenings to help the action on its way.

Ibsen after his travels abroad in 1852 adopted the intrigue technique wholeheartedly as far as the action was concerned. But, as we can see in his earliest dramas, his plays were based on a fate *motif*, inherited in part from romantic tradition, in part from a protestant upbringing with all its insistence on individual responsibility for sin and the inevitable retribution that follows. The causal relationship of sin and retribution embodied in the concept of fate stands in direct opposition to the belief that human actions are controlled by chance, and Ibsen's development as a dramatist is marked by the way in which the chance factor is gradually eliminated by the fate factor in the action. This change was assisted by contact with the ideas which inspired the naturalistic writers, with their deterministic belief in the firmness of natural laws and causality. In France Henri Becque was the only dramatist who reacted successfully against the intrigue tradition, while other authors resorted to the novel, where accepted traditions of form were not so strong. Ibsen was the first dramatist of European significance to break with the artificial technique of French intrigue drama, though a substratum of the old forms is traceable in the action and dialogue of nearly all his plays.

Ibsen's acquaintance with French repertoire dates from 1850, when he came to Christiania, and one of his earliest criticisms spoke scornfully of 'Scribe and Co.'s dramatic sweetmeats'. But on his tour abroad in 1852 he appreciated the effectiveness of Scribe on the stage and bought several of his plays for the Bergen theatre, where thirty per cent of the works he produced were written by this author. As late as 1861 we find him defending the inclusion of Scribe in the repertoire of the Norwegian theatre in Christiania. An examination of his work as a whole shows that he retained much of the Scribe technique in his later plays, though by the time he had written *Ghosts* in 1881 he had abandoned almost completely the French use of situation.

Let us first consider the artificialities of the French technique which Ibsen early adopted but subsequently eliminated in his plays. All Ibsen's early plays are centred round conspiracies, plots or intrigues of some kind and the action is continually referred to by the characters as resembling a game of chess or cards, just as we find in Scribe's play, his *Contes de la Reine de*

Navarre, a work produced by Ibsen in Bergen (October 1854). We meet this image in Ibsen's first play *Catilina* (S.D.V. 1, 48) and from 1852 onwards it recurs with great frequency. In *Lady Inger* we find references to chess, cards, betting, and words like 'trap' and 'snare' are often repeated in the dialogue. In *The Warriors of Helgeland* Sigurd challenges Gunnar to a duel with the words 'It will be a game of chess for life and death'. Similarly in *The Pretenders* the second act opens with Skule playing chess with the arch-intriguer Bishop Nikolas. *The League of Youth* is full of references to 'the game', 'playing cards', and one of the situations of the play is brought about by a game of forfeits. With the next play, *Emperor and Galilean*, the intrigue element is completely lacking together with the accompanying imagery and symbolism. From now on Ibsen seriously attempted to eliminate intrigue from all his plays and the themes no longer consist of thickening plots and conspiracies.

Ibsen's plays are nearest the French model when their endings are the same, these endings which consist of unmasking the villain, recompensing the hero and uniting him at last with his lady love. *Pillars of Society* is the last play of Ibsen's to make free use of the artificially happy ending, and with *A Doll's House* he breaks the French tradition. Misunderstandings of various kinds, both verbal ones and those depending on mistaken identity, were also freely used by Ibsen after 1852 and appear for the first time in *Midsummer Eve*, where they are used for comic effect. They are used for dramatic effect to a large extent in *Lady Inger, The Feast at Solhaug* and *Olaf Liljekrans*; they are omitted in *The Warriors of Helgeland*, reduced to three in *Love's Comedy*, after which they are completely absent in Ibsen's work except in the case of *The League of Youth*, the last offshoot of French comedy with Ibsen. Only once again in *The Lady from the Sea* did Ibsen resort to misunderstanding for the development of the action.

Intrigue drama made much use of coincidence and unmotivated happenings to clear up situations or to complicate them. The same was the case with the various types of *deus ex machinâ* employed by Ibsen in early plays, particularly the unexpected entry of a character at the moment when he is called for, the type of entry we find caricatured in *The Master Builder*, when Hilde comes in as soon as Solness prophesies that 'youth will come knocking at the door'. In *Olaf Liljekrans* the hero opportunely arrives at the eleventh hour to save the life of his bride and bring about a happy ending. Ibsen later altered the function of the entry and used it in order to introduce unexpected characters who broke off a thread of conversation and thus increased the suspense of the exposition.

Side by side with these happy coincidences and entries on demand we find a similar use of artificial tools such as papers and documents, potions, poisons, lost rings and trinkets. These play a large part in the complication or elucidation of situations, and again make their entry into Ibsen's work in 1852. The whole action of *Midsummer Eve* revolves around some lost documents and the effects of a magic potion. In *Lady Inger* a conventional recognition scene is brought about at the end when the heroine identifies her dead son by the help of a ring he wears round his neck, and here the action also is artificially stimulated with secret papers. In *The Feast at Solhaug* a goblet of poisoned mead creates situation after situation until it is finally emptied out of the window, and in *The Warriors of Helgeland* the crisis is brought to a climax when Dagny shows Hjørdis the bracelet which the latter gave Sigurd, believing him to have been her husband Gunnar. There is an exciting letter of identity in *The Pretenders* and a note of hand in *The League of Youth*, but here the use of these devices stops except in two outstanding instances, the fatal letter in *A Doll's House* which creates such an atmosphere of tension, and the letters in *Little Eyolf*, which in a feebly conventional manner prove that Asta was after all not Allmers's half-sister.

The most striking element of intrigue drama adopted by Ibsen was the stereotyped scenes and situations which he used after 1852. Until the introduction of the tragic ending in *A Doll's House*, the endings of his plays, as we have seen, were always associated with conventional settlements of various kinds. *The League of Youth*, for instance, ends with three betrothals, one conversion and one unmasking and punishment. Scenes and situations of this kind are later abolished at the end of his plays, but Ibsen always made full use of other types which were current in intrigue drama. The scenes between Nora and her children in *A Doll's House* before and after her meeting with the money-lender Krogstad are a perfect pastiche of scenes from Dumas fils.

Again there are the recognition scenes. Scribe was very fond

83

of using recognition scenes and these were not always placed at the end. One of his plays, *Les Prèmieres Amours*, which had been searchingly analysed and commended by Kierkegaard, turns upon the meeting of old school friends, just like the meeting of Gregers and Hjalmar in *The Wild Duck*. Ibsen's plays frequently depend on the meeting of old friends or enemies who settle old grievances or keep old promises. From *Pillars of Society* onwards the recognition and meeting become almost a fixed convention of his technique and are particularly useful in helping out the retrospective exposition which he now adopts. Old friends meet and discuss old times and the action is set in motion by the conflict of past and present. These scenes take the same course from the entry of Lona Hessel in *Pillars of Society* to the sudden appearance of Irene in Ibsen's last play.

The other conventional scene adopted and developed by Ibsen was the *scène à faire*, the scene in which the two conflicting parties make a final reckoning. Lady Inger squares her account in a Shakespearean monologue, Nora sits down to lecture Helmer with the words, 'This is going to be a final settlement, Torvald', and Ellida stands between the stranger and her husband to make her final choice. This type of scene is repeated again and again towards the end of Ibsen's plays and it is in fact only the natural fluency of the dialogues which distinguish them from the scenes we find with Augier and Dumas fils.

One last feature which links Ibsen's work with that of the intrigue dramatists is his use of a secret and its revelation, round which to construct his plays. His most characteristic intrigue-plays are full of them. Lady Inger has a secret past which is revealed, the same is the case with Nils Lykke and Nils Stenssøn, and there are a secret passage and secret documents, while Olaf Skaktavl's identity at first is kept secret. In conformity with the concentration and simplification of the action in Ibsen's later work the secrets are in most cases reduced to a minimum, but Ibsen uses the same technique of increasing the suspense by delaying the final revelation as long as possible, and this is particularly the case when the retrospective method of exposition is adopted.

But Ibsen was by no means entirely dependent on intrigue technique for the shaping of the action in his plays. In his modern plays he evolved an individual method of treatment characterized by his particular form of exposition and ending, two features which will be discussed separately later, by his strict observation of the unities, and by economy of structure, both in the reduction of the number of characters and the elimination of sub-plots and superfluities. In *Pillars of Society* we meet the first play in which unity of place is introduced. Originally Ibsen had planned four separate scenes and these were subsequently condensed into one. Sub-plots were not eliminated until 1881 with the writing of *Ghosts*, but later with *The Lady from the Sea* they were introduced again with the object of throwing the main plot into relief by contrast. Only in one play, *John Gabriel Borkman*, is complete unity of time observed and here the action progresses without a pause between the acts. But with his modern plays Ibsen always restricts the action to the course of about a day, just as had been the case with the majority of his earlier plays. Only five of Ibsen's plays extend the action beyond the bounds of weeks, months and years: *Catilina*, *The Pretenders*, *Brand*, *Peer Gynt* and *Emperor and Galilean*. The rest of his works are restricted to an average limit of forty-eight hours, while his most consciously realistic plays have an even more limited period. *A Doll's House* was originally planned to cover a period from Christmas Eve till New Year's Day, but was reduced finally to three days. *Ghosts* covers only a span of a few hours from the late afternoon of one day till the dawn of the next. This shortening of the time interval was also bound up with the adoption of retrospective exposition, which permitted the play to begin at a crisis and the main action to be relegated to the past.

The same tendency to concentration and economy we find in the number of acts, the restriction of the characters and the elimination of superfluities from the dialogue. From the writing of *Love's Comedy* onwards Ibsen abandoned the French tradition of dividing his acts into scenes according to the entrances and exits of the characters, and in his modern plays he generally abandoned the classical convention of five acts and restricted the length of his plays to four or three. (Among his later plays only *An Enemy of the People*, *The Wild Duck* and *The Lady from the Sea* have five acts.) In his earlier plays Ibsen was accustomed to mustering a large number of characters. His gigantic work, *Emperor and Galilean*, has no fewer than thirty-three speaking parts in the first half and some forty-five in the second. The first of his series of modern plays, *Pillars of Society*, also has a large cast of nineteen, but the number is reduced in *A Doll's House*, and in *Ghosts* there are only five, while the action is to all intents and purposes carried on with only three. The same classical economy and concentration is observable in nearly all Ibsen's later plays, though he never achieves such simplicity as Strindberg with his monodrama, *The Stronger*, or his duologues. Superfluous characters are eliminated in the course of composition, but many of the characters play their part in the action of the play though they have been suppressed entirely, such as the dead Captain Alving in *Ghosts*, the dead wife Beate in *Rosmersholm* and Gregers Werle's dead mother in *The Wild Duck*. This same concentration and elimination applies as well to the dialogue.

While the action in Ibsen's later plays is reduced to a minimum and for the most part is relegated to the past with the help of the retrospective method of exposition, the fate *motif* begins to dominate and to exclude the element of chance which pervaded his earlier plays. With Schiller and the romantics fate was but another name for chance. The fatal dates and daggers in the plays of Werner and Grillparzer are pure coincidences and nothing more. We meet survivals of this fate-concept in Ibsen's earlier plays, the fatal ring in *Lady Inger*, the fatal cup in *The Feast at Solhaug*, the fatal bracelet of *The Warriors of Helgeland*. A parody of these fate symbols we find in the fatal pistol in *The Wild Duck* which played its part in the Ekdal family history, the pistol with which both Ekdal and Hjalmar had been too cowardly to commit suicide and which was finally used for that purpose by Hedvig. But Ibsen's use of fate was in accordance with the Greek conception of fate as standing in a direct relationship to guilt and not identical with chance, coinciding with his protestant moral upbringing, which stressed the doctrine of retribution for past misdeeds. Parallel conceptions were held independently by two other great Scandinavians: Carl Linné who discussed the whole problem in an unpublished essay, *Nemesis Divina*; and Strindberg, who partly inherited the conception from Linné, partly developed it independently in accordance with this religious experience. Linné was significantly enough not only a classical scholar, but also the son of a protestant minister, and Strindberg passed his childhood in an atmosphere of austere pietism. Childhood experiences obviously left their mark in the case of these two Swedes and the same we can imagine in the case of Ibsen with his religious mother, his moralistic outlook and his profound knowledge of the Bible.

Fate with Ibsen always has a moral significance; he never accepted the bare amoral determinism of the naturalistic school. It is definitely conceived as a power which metes out inexorable punishment for sin, whereas with the naturalistic school sin and guilt were abolished from the vocabulary, as with Strindberg who at one period (Preface to *Lady Julia*) wrote, 'The naturalist has abolished the word guilt together with God'. Thus in *Ghosts* the realistic *motif* of venereal disease is only a cloak for the old testament doctrine of the visitation of the sins of the fathers, and the real centre of the tragedy is Mrs. Alving, who is punished for having married a man with money whom she did not love.

This type of old testament fate plays its part in all Ibsen's work, though it does not gain control of the action until we come to his later plays, when the retrospective exposition is used to unearth past sins and the plays end with retribution and not with a revelation. Ibsen's first play, *Catilina*, is full of references to fate and Nemesis, and the hero is punished for the sin of seducing Furia's sister. The plays that follow contain many references to fate though it is chance which brings about the final catastrophes. Lady Inger, for instance, falls a victim to her past sins and Nils Lykke, like Catilina, is haunted by fate when he falls in love with the sister of the woman he has seduced. In *The Warriors of Helgeland* we meet with the first play in which Ibsen abandons chance altogether and adopts fate in the control of the action. Here, in spite of the artificiality of prophetic verses which are fulfilled, the 'web of the Norns' enmeshes the characters in the typical Ibsen manner. Sigurd has betrayed Hjørdis in the past and married another woman, for which sin he meets his end. This is a typical formula for Ibsen's tragedies which begin with *Ghosts*. His conception of sin is exaggerated till it includes not only sinful actions but sinful thoughts, as in *The Master Builder*, where Solness meets his doom because of a half-uttered wish. As Ibsen grows older and his work becomes more and more autobiographical and his own past haunts his conscience more and more, the sins which envelop the action of his plays are set in a progressively remoter past until the plays take on the character of an armchair conversation, recalling forgotten memories and waiting for the hand of fate to mete out its punishment in the last act: With age, Ibsen became more and more pessimistic, and denied the capacity of human freewill to flaunt destiny. Nora is the last of Ibsen's characters to face her past and start over again, with the exception of Ellida, who dares to make a free choice, and Allmers and Rita, who decide to make the best of things. The rest of his characters are the victims of their own past and are crushed by the weight of the corpses which they carry on their backs.

The logic of Ibsen's fate *motif* is of course purely fictitious, but it creates an illusion of realism in the moralistic atmosphere of his plays and eliminates the element of chance. The adoption of this fate *motif* was the primary factor in excluding the intrigue technique from his plays, and we have seen how in his modern tragedies, where it dominates, the survival of the conventions of French social drama are very few. It is partly the inheritance of a guilty nonconformist conscience, partly a survival of romantic pathos, but it is presented in realistic modern dress and satisfies the demands of illusion.

CHAPTER VI

THE EXPOSITION

IN primitive drama exposition is bound to be crude, as with the Greeks and with the medieval church drama, because the play represents myths or legends which are already known to the spectators, and therefore the devices of suspense and surprising revelation are unnecessary. The exposition in these cases took the form of direct narrative. It survived in literary drama until the eighteenth century and can be seen on the popular stage at the present day. 'I am the villain of the piece', followed by a roll of drums and purple lights, one of the conventions of exposition in Victorian melodrama, is of exactly the same nature as the narrative introduction in morality plays. 'Asides', stage whispers and explanatory monologues are a form of this primitive narrative exposition in literary drama.

The monologue exposition, a form of introductory prologue, lived on after the middle ages in the literary comedies of Holberg, in Lessing's and Goethe's drama and in Scribe's plays, so that we are not surprised to find Ibsen's first play, *Catilina*, following the same principles. The transition from religious to secular drama was, however, accompanied by a new demand for realistic illusion, and in obedience to these demands the naïve narrative exposition tended to become more sophisticated and realistic. D'Aubignac advised the French classical dramatists to avoid the monologue and to use, other devices, such as confidants, conversations between master and servant, and discussions between servants alone.

Ibsen makes use of confidants very frequently. Mrs. Linde is Nora's confidant in *A Doll's House*, and Dr. Herdal acts as Solness's confidant in *The Master Builder*. But the *pièce à thèse* in France had already transformed the confidant into the *raisonneur* character. The raisonneur-confidant recurs often with Ibsen in his modern plays: Dr. Rank in *A Doll's House* and Dr. Relling in *The Wild Duck* are two outstanding examples. But in his later work Ibsen eliminated these mouthpiece characters almost entirely, beginning with *Rosmersholm*. Confidences between master and servant were a traditional element of *bourgeois* drama and more particularly of comedy. This method of exposition occurs twice with Ibsen in his modern plays, in *Hedda Gabler* and *Rosmersholm*. Conversations between servants alone, as in the case of *Romeo and Juliet*, are used for the purposes of exposition by the great majority of dramatists, and were particularly favoured by Goethe and Schiller and the German domestic dramatists Iffland and Kotzebue. Ibsen adopted this type very early in *Lady Inger*, where it is obviously inspired by Shakespeare, and later on in *The Wild Duck*, where Pettersen the butler and a hired servant from outside clumsily recapitulate the preamble to the Werle-Ekdal family history before the guests leave the dining-room after dinner. This is Ibsen's nearest approach to the ungainly method so much exploited by Dumas fils of letting characters tell one another things they obviously know already. Such expositions are usually avoided by Ibsen.

In avoiding direct narration, exposition came to depend very largely on allusion, direct or indirect, or on inadvertent remarks. In *The Merchant of Venice* Portia's love for Bassanio is confirmed by a slip of the tongue when she says (Act III, Sc. 2):

> 'One half of me is yours, the other half yours,
> Mine own, I would say.'

S. Freud has pointed out a similar instance in Schiller's *Wallenstein*. Subtleties of this nature are also used by Ibsen. In *Rosmersholm* Rosmer reveals his intimate relations with Rebekka when he, in the presence of Rector Kroll, refers to Rebekka by her Christian name and then corrects himself to 'Miss West'. Allusions are also necessary not only for the revelation of relationships between people but to preserve the continuity of the action. The unity of action in *Ghosts*, for instance, is a result of the suspense and expectancy aroused by breaking off questions and postponing their answers till the ensuing act. Act II is closely bound to Act I by the question asked by Manders at the end of the latter, concerning Regine's identity. This is revealed in Act II and the action is accelerated until it is checked at the end of the act by another question. Will Mrs. Alving have the courage to free herself from the ghosts that haunt her and tell the truth to Osvald without ideals suffering in consequence? In Act III she tells the ungarnished truth, only to find that her ideals of uprightness were only another ghost, and the play ends with the tense question of whether she will be able to rid herself of this last obsession and give Osvald the fatal dose of morphia.

Continuity of time is preserved in *The Wild Duck* without the necessity of descriptive stage directions. In Act III Gina says to Hjalmar: 'I am only expecting the two sweethearts who are to be taken together . . . I booked them an appointment for this after-noon when you'll be having your nap.' Act IV opens with Gina at the door saying good-bye to her clients on the stairs, and the room is so arranged that one can see a photograph has just been taken. Thus without any further indication we realize that the act begins on the afternoon of the same day as Act III. Ibsen's method of exposition is always most careful in preserving the continuity of acts by allusions such as these.

The most characteristic feature of Ibsen's technique of exposition is, however, his use of what may be called the retrospective method, a technique employed by Sophocles, by Racine and to a certain extent by Hebbel. That is to say, he prefers to begin his tragedy just before the catastrophe and to make the dialogue unravel the preceding events in retrospect, instead of presenting the actual events in succession on the stage. This type of exposition concentrates the action into a very small space of time, in con-formity with the realistic desire to observe the unities. It is also, as it happens, a type of exposition favoured by the traditional fate-tragedy, the dramatic conflict in all cases being between past and present, the sins of the past contrasting violently with the calm atmosphere of the present and swiftly destroying the idyll as retribution approaches. The dramatic contrast between the beginnings and endings of Ibsen's plays is dependent for its effect on this type of exposition. In *Pillars of Society* the false atmo-sphere of calm at the sewing party is dispersed as the past is revealed step by step and brings about the fall of the self-righteous consul. In *Ghosts* the play opens with Regine watering flowers, in *Rosmers-holm* Rebekka is arranging flowers in the morning-room as the curtain rises, and in *Hedda Gabler* Aunt Julia arrives in the first scene to greet the young married couple with a bouquet. Nothing could however be more characteristic of Ibsen than the endings of these plays, Osvald going mad, Rebekka and Rosmer throwing themselves into the mill-race, and Hedda shooting herself.

The first instance of this type of exposition is to be found in the historical play *Warriors of Helgeland* (1857), though the dramatic revelations of many of the earlier plays concern past sins. The method was then dropped and not used again until 1877 with *Pillars of Society*. From now on, with one exception, in the comedy *An Enemy of the People*, Ibsen never abandons this technique and he evolves a formula for its application which is particularly characteristic of his style. He presents first of all an idyllic picture of a household living its everyday life. Then this little fenced-in world is suddenly broken into by a visitor from the world outside. He or she is an old friend of the family who has not been seen for several years. These meetings of old friends are the pivot of nearly all Ibsen's plays and they are followed up by a perfectly natural exchange of recollections and inquiries about the intervening period during which the friends have not seen one another. It is these inquiries which open up old wounds and bring about the catastrophe. An exposition of this nature is obviously more realistic than most since it eliminates the necessity of asides and explanatory monologues, because the characters can tell one another what they otherwise would have to communicate direct to the audience. It can also deal with almost unlimited periods of time and extensions of space without exerting the spectator's imagination to any great extent. In plays like *Pillars of Society*, *Ghosts*, *Hedda Gabler* and *When We Dead Awaken*, although the drama is enacted in a restricted space (in the same room in the first three, in the same district in the last) the action actually concerns not only local events, but happenings in America, Paris, a European tour, and on the Starnberger See. The time extension is also great, and becomes progressively greater as Ibsen himself grows older and feels the power of the past over his conscience. The earlier modern plays concern young people, while the later plays are definitely based on a conflict of youth and age, so that in Ibsen's last work we find the old sculptor atoning for sins which he had committed as a very young man.

There are certain technical difficulties, of course, in this type of exposition which Ibsen often found it hard to surmount. Persons who have not met for a long time are inclined to involve themselves in explanations which would be tedious on the stage and would hold up the action. Dumas fils and Scribe had a ready solution by which they made them into schoolfriends. Ibsen, however, simplified this by very often relating the characters to one another so that there is no need of introduction. The mechanism creaks at points, and the cold light of reason reveals improbabilities which are hidden to an absorbed audience. In *The Wild Duck*, for instance, Gregers has not seen Hjalmar for seventeen years, and his warm friendship is a little hard to explain when we realize that he knows nothing of Hjalmar's occupation, nor of his wife or their fifteen year old daughter; but Ibsen here covers his tracks by allusions to a correspondence between them which has come to a standstill.

This type of exposition is also helped out by the device of repetition which has already been referred to when discussing the use of fate, the fatal objects, words and actions which are associated with the repetition of fatal catastrophes. Heredity also plays its part here, as in *The Wild Duck*, where Ibsen at the last moment introduced the element of Hedvig's weak eyesight, which immediately refers the spectator to Werle's weak eyes and arouses the suspicion, which is later confirmed, that Hedvig is Werle's illegitimate daughter. In this case Ibsen makes very effective use of dramatic irony. In Act II Hjalmar tells Gregers that Hedvig may become blind. Gregers asks him to explain it and Hjalmar remarks with a sigh: 'Heredity, of course.' Gregers starts back and exclaims, 'Heredity!' thinking with the audience of his own weak-sighted father. But Hjalmar has no suspicions and attributes Hedvig's bad eyesight to her great grandmother, not realizing the real connection until the end of the fourth act. Previously the only clues were to be found by doing a little mental arithmetic with the dates of Hjalmar's marriage and Hedvig's birth. In the same way, in *Rosmersholm*, the fact that Rebekka is Dr. West's illegitimate daughter is demonstrated indirectly by a comparison of dates. The skilful use of allusion is seen again in the latter play when we realize how Rebekka has unwittingly committed incest and been her father's mistress, solely from her expression of unspeakable horror when Dr. West is revealed as her father. A brilliant use of allusion is seen again in the case of *Hedda Gabler*, in which play Hedda's pregnancy is communicated to the spectator without any direct reference, simply by Hedda's behaviour and her annoyance when Tesman compliments her on getting plump. It is not till some time after that Aunt Julia and later Tesman realize her condition and mention it in veiled language. Allusion again is all-important in *The Wild Duck*, for the duck itself is hardly seen and only gains significance by allusion and description.

Ibsen's manipulation of exits and entrances also assists the exposition and increases the suspense of the gradual revelations. In the drawing-room drama of Ibsen's predecessors, new characters were introduced in order to help out the action by bringing in a letter, taking a message or imparting new information. Ibsen introduces new characters in order to break off the conversation and create suspense by putting off revelations until the catastrophe is due. Traces of this method can be found in his early Bergen work, but it was not evolved to technical perfection until the writing of *Emperor and Galilean*. Instances in the later plays abound. Reference has already been made to the suspense caused by the endings of the acts in *Ghosts*. A similar suspense is brought about by the entrances in *The Lady from the Sea*. Lyngstrand comes in and breaks off the conversation between Ellida and Arnholm just as she is about to confide her strange obsessions to him; just as Ellida is going to tell Wangel about the stranger she is broken off by Bolette and the arrival of the excursion party. Not until the end of the act does she reveal the extent of her fears to Wangel, and then with the arrival of the stranger in the third act the drama begins to develop unchecked. In *Rosmersholm* the action is punctuated by the two appearances of Rosmer's old tutor Brendel, the first at the beginning of the play, which starts the catastrophe, the second at the end, when he gives Rosmer and Rebekka the solution to their dilemma by his indirect references to suicide. These exits and entrances are always well motivated in the later plays, and the characters have given up their tendency to turn up on demand as they did previously.

In order to comprehend the full skill of Ibsen's exposition it is easiest to consider one play in its entirety. *The Wild Duck* is excellent for this purpose, as it is a good example of Ibsen's mature technique. This play covers a period of almost two days on the stage, but the action is taken as representing the precipitation of a tragedy which has been ripening for over seventeen years. The catalyst in the play is Gregers Werle, who returns after having been away for seventeen years. Gradually, by his questions and conversations with various characters, the past is unveiled, a hidden sin is revealed and finds its drastic retribution in the suicide of the little illegitimate girl Hedvig. The action progresses by a series of references to the past which are accompanied by allusions to four other factors. These are namely, Werle's weak eyesight, Hedvig's weak eyesight, the suggestive presence of the duck and the fatal pistol, and they bring about the immediate tragedy. Suspense is achieved by putting off revelations, which are interrupted by the entrance of a character or the end of an act. The time factors and the other four factors referred to are represented on the accompanying chart, which shows diagrammatically how the action progresses by repeated digressions and allusions. The continually interrupted references to the past do not give a full picture of what has happened until Relling describes Hjalmar's youth to Gregers in the beginning of the last act, and then it is left to the last two factors, the wild duck itself and the fatal pistol, to consummate the tragedy in the present.

The following analysis of *The Wild Duck* traces the development of the action as it is diagrammatically presented on the chart:

ACT I. *Werle's drawing-room. Evening.*

Two servants are talking. Werle is celebrating the return of his son Gregers by a dinner-party. Old Ekdal passes through the room to the office, and we learn that this broken old man has once been a lieutenant and previously Werle's business partner, but that he has served a term of imprisonment for some mysterious timber speculation of an illicit nature. He now does copying work for Werle.

The guests leave the dining-room and pass on into the music-room.

Gregers and Hjalmar remain behind. They recall old times and ask questions. They have not met for 17 years. After the disaster to his father, Ekdal, Hjalmar had to abandon his studies and took up photography for a living, with the financial assistance of Gregers's father. On his instigation also he married Gina, Werle's housekeeper, who had looked after the household during Mrs. Werle's fatal illness.

The guests return. We notice Werle has weak eyes and cannot stand the light. They exchange witticisms and Hjalmar is ridiculed.

Old Ekdal, who has been unable to escape from the office, now makes his way out through the room and causes extreme embarrassment to Werle and Hjalmar by his presence. Hjalmar leaves. Mrs. Sørby takes the guests to another room.

Hjalmar's youth

Ekdal's past, 17 years earlier

Werle's past

Gina's past

Hjalmar's marriage, almost 15 years earlier

Hedvig's birth, 14 years earlier

Werle's weak eyesight

Hedvig's weak eyesight

Allusions to Wild Duck

Allusions to Pistol

ACT I. Werle's drawing room

The same evening

ACT II

Next morning

ACT III

Hjalmar's studio

Evening

ACT IV

Morning of Hedvig's birthday

ACT V

Chart of the action in *The Wild Duck*

Gregers is left alone with his father and reproaches him for leaving the Ekdals destitute. Werle protests that he assists them as far as is compatible with his position without arousing suspicion. Ekdal does copying work for the office, and Werle has made it financially possible for Hjalmar to become a photographer and to marry. Gregers accuses his father of having had illicit relations with Gina and of having disposed of her conveniently by marrying her off to Hjalmar. Werle attributes these rumours to his late wife's neurotic jealousy, denies them and offers Gregers a partnership in the family firm. Gregers suspects a hidden motive, finds his father intends to marry his housekeeper, Mrs. Sørby, decides to leave his father's house for good and announces his intention of fulfilling his life's mission. Curtain. (Suspense caused by Gregers's refusal to say what his mission is.)

ACT II. *Hjalmar's studio. Same evening.*

Gina and Hedvig, the 14 year old daughter, are waiting for Hjalmar to come home. Hedvig is peering with her weak eyes over a book. They discuss household affairs.

Old Ekdal comes home with his work and a bottle of drink concealed in his pocket. Before going into his room he opens the door of the garret and exclaims: 'They're all asleep. She's lying in her basket.' (First veiled allusion to the duck.)

While the women are discussing him Ekdal comes in again and fetches hot water from the kitchen to make himself a drink, under the pretext of using it to dissolve his clotted ink.

Hjalmar returns from the party, Ekdal enters again and they all listen while Hjalmar boasts of his social success and disappoints Hedvig by having forgotten to bring any tit-bits, consoling her instead with the menu. He talks to his father about the inhabitants of the attic (suspense of veiled language) and Ekdal then returns to his room for a drink, pretending to clean his pipe.

Hjalmar then becomes testy, but is soothed by beer and food and finally consents to play the flute.

This idyllic family scene is then broken into by Gregers, who is given a hearty welcome. (Arrival of the messenger from the outside world and transformation of idyll into catastrophe.) Hjalmar confides to him that Hedvig is in danger of becoming blind and that her ailment is hereditary. Gregers thinks immediately of his own father, but Hjalmar is referring to Hedvig's great-grandmother. They eat sandwiches and drink beer. Hjalmar tells Gregers that Hedvig is fourteen and that her birthday is in two days' time. He also explains rather awkwardly, but with a certain sense of sly pride, that he has been married fifteen years all but a few months. Old Ekdal enters and they all sit down and eat together.

Ekdal then goes and opens the garret to show Gregers the wonders it contains, and points out in the dark the pigeons and rabbits and the wild duck in its basket. The doors are then shut. (First direct allusion to the duck.)

The duck was wounded by Werle out shooting and it was given to Ekdal by the butler. Ekdal goes to sleep. Gregers agrees to rent one of Gina's rooms as a lodger and, using Ekdal's words, he expresses his desire to be a well-trained retriever so as to bring wounded wild duck to the surface when they dive to the bottom. Exeunt Gregers and Hjalmar.

Gina is puzzled, but Hedvig suspects a meaning in Gregers's symbolical language. Hjalmar returns full of satisfaction at having got his old friend as a lodger, and in spite of Gina's premonitions of disaster he assures her of a bright future.

ACT III. *Hjalmar's studio. Next morning.*

Hjalmar tells Gina that Gregers and the two other lodgers, Dr. Relling and Molvik, are coming to breakfast. He sits down grudgingly to touch up photographs. Ekdal enters and they persuade one another to stop working and to play in the garret instead. They open the doors and it is revealed in full sunshine. (Only view of garret and inhabitants in whole play.) The floor and inhabitants of the garret are then concealed from view by a sail-cloth to keep the animals from straying. The upper part is visible through a fishing net. Ekdal enters the garret.

Gina comes in to lay breakfast and Hjalmar immediately insists on using the table for his work. Gina leaves and Hedvig comes in, persuades her father to join Ekdal in the garret and help him move the duck's trough. She asks to do the photographs for him and he consents when she promises not to strain her eyes. Hjalmar goes.

Gregers enters and talks to Hedvig. They discuss the garret, she tells him of the strange things she has found there, says she often thinks of it as the bottom of the sea. He asks her the strange question if she is quite sure that it is not the bottom of the sea, and Gina enters and breaks off their conversation. (Suspense.)

The table is laid and a shot is suddenly fired in the attic. (First allusion to pistol.) Hjalmar comes out with a smoking pistol and tells Hedvig not to touch it as one of the barrels is loaded. He lays it on a shelf and Gregers looks into the garret and describes the duck which is invisible to the audience. (Allusion.)

Gina and Hedvig go out and leave Hjalmar and Gregers alone. The doors of the garret are shut. Hjalmar confides to Gregers that he leaves to his wife the menial work of the photography business because he himself is occupied with an important photographic invention of a very vague nature with which to fulfil his life's mission, namely the rehabilitation of the family name. He describes the sufferings of his father's disgrace and tells of the fatal pistol with which he and his father had both almost committed suicide. Instead of ending his life he had determined to dedicate it to a mission, to make the name of Ekdal famous by his invention and to make it possible for his father to wear his uniform again. He takes a nap after lunch every day, and hopes for inspiration while his faith in himself is supported by the encouragement of the lodger Dr. Relling. Gregers is just about to tell Hjalmar the truth when he is interrupted by Gina and Hedvig bringing in the breakfast and the arrival of the guests Relling and Molvik. (Suspense.)

The latter have been on the razzle the night before, and when Ekdal emerges from the garret with a newly flayed rabbit-skin Molvik's stomach is turned and he has to leave the table. Relling flatters Hjalmar, who preens himself on his family happiness, while Gregers protests. Relling threatens to eject Gregers if he will not hold his tongue, the latter turns to leave and at the door meets his father (surprise), who asks to speak to him alone. The others withdraw discreetly.

Werle refers to the mission of which Gregers had spoken in his last conversation and warns him that he will not help Hjalmar by revealing to him the circumstances of his marriage. Gregers refuses to renounce his mission and Werle leaves.

The others return and Gregers expresses a wish to go out for a walk with Hjalmar. Relling advises against such a course, but Hjalmar goes and Hedvig is left perplexed at all the inexplicable complications.

99

ACT IV. *Hjalmar's studio. Afternoon of same day.*

Gina and Hedvig are waiting for Hjalmar to return from his walk. Hjalmar enters. He has been enlightened about the past by Gregers. He is peevish and touchy and threatens to strangle the wild duck, a gift soiled by Werle's hands. He promises the distressed Hedvig, however, that he will refrain and tells her to go out and get some fresh air.

Hjalmar faces Gina alone (*scène à faire*) and she confesses to her former relations with Werle.

Gregers enters in high spirits, but is distressed when he finds that his action has not met with the desired result.

Relling comes in and curses Gregers for his interference and begs them all at any rate to be careful of Hedvig who is at the strange and impressionable age of puberty.

Mrs. Sørby breaks in upon them, announces that she is leaving in order to get married to Werle. Relling, an old flame of hers, leaves dejected and invites Hjalmar to join him and Molvik in a drinking bout to drown their sorrows. Mrs. Sørby explains Werle's need of a wife because of his approaching blindness. Hjalmar is surprised, and she goes with his assurances that he intends to repay with interest all that he has received from Werle and to assert his independence. Gregers praises Hjalmar for his moral idealism and Hjalmar expresses a sense of regret that Werle, and not he, should finally contract the ideal marriage.

Hedvig comes in, Mrs. Sørby has given her a present which she is not to open till her birthday. Hjalmar insists on opening it on the spot and it turns out to contain a deed of gift to Hedvig from Werle. Hedvig reads it and at the sight of her weak eyes Hjalmar sees her relationship to Werle; he becomes frantic and she is told harshly to get out of his sight and go out of the room. He tears the deed of gift in half, and then challenges Gina, asking if Hedvig is his child or no. She confesses she is uncertain, he decides to leave the house. Hedvig's distressed pleadings are unheard and Hjalmar stamps out of the room. Gina follows him and Gregers is left alone with Hedvig.

Gregers suggests to Hedvig that she will regain her father's affection if she sacrifices the duck for him. Gina comes back to say that Hjalmar has gone out with Relling and Molvik, and Gregers leaves with a reminder to Hedvig to remember the duck.

ACT V. *Hjalmar's studio. The morning of Hedvig's birthday.*

Old Ekdal goes into the garret, and Gina and Hedvig are waiting for Hjalmar to come back. Gregers comes to inquire after him and Relling enters to say that he is asleep, snoring in his room. Gina and Hedvig exit and leave Gregers and Relling alone.

Relling undermines Gregers's belief in Hjalmar's ideal personality, and analyses him as the product of an upbringing by two maiden aunts, of admiration by those around him; a conglomerate of other people's ideas and expressions, a person who cannot survive without illusion as the stimulating principle of life. Hedvig enters and Relling leaves.

Gregers reminds Hedvig of his suggestion about sacrificing the duck and he leaves as Ekdal emerges from the garret. Hedvig asks him the best way to shoot a duck and he tells her. He goes into his room and she fingers with the pistol on the shelf and replaces it as her mother comes in. Hedvig goes to see to the coffee in the kitchen, and Hjalmar at last enters.

He has come to collect his belongings before leaving for good, and rejects all Hedvig's advances when she looks out of the kitchen. He turns his back on her and goes into his room, followed by Gina.

Hedvig in despair suddenly remembers her promise to Gregers, exclaims, 'the wild duck', takes the pistol from the shelf and hurries into the garret.

Hjalmar and Gina return. He looks for his pistol, finds it has gone and supposes his father is using it in the garret. He proceeds to eat the food which Gina has prepared, then decides to remain at home a day or so, and finally sets about sticking together the deed of gift which he had torn the day before.

Gregers enters and Gina leaves. He assures Hjalmar of Hedvig's devotion and promises that he will be given proof of it; Hjalmar in turn expresses his affection for Hedvig, but demands a sign. He wonders what answer she would give if she were asked to sacrifice her life for his. A shot is heard from the garret. (Dramatic irony.) Gregers utters an exclamation of joy believing that she has persuaded Old Ekdal to shoot her duck. But suddenly the old man comes out of his room. They then open the doors and find that she has not shot the duck but herself.

Relling responds to their cries for assistance and states that she is dead. The drunk Molvik enters and lends an atmosphere of macabre humour to the scene. Hjalmar and Gina, united in their sorrow, carry out the corpse and leave Relling to pronounce a cynical epilogue in his last words to Gregers, the bungling idealist.

The Wild Duck gives a good example of Ibsen's method of exposition, and his expositions are some of the most characteristic features of his technique. In his use of monologues and asides his general tendency is to evolve realistic conventions. In the treatment of the general features of his exposition this tendency has also been obvious. What we now accept as plain conventions, the retrospective analysis, the manipulation of exits, extrances and curtains to cause suspense and tension, the idyllic beginning and the drastic ending, the use of the meeting and the introduction of the conventional character from the world outside, these were all conventions adopted in the name of realistic illusion, and these conventions were elaborated in conscious reaction to an equally rigid form that had dominated the theatre previously. Ibsen's method of exposition was of great consequence for the theatre of his successors, and it was adopted wholesale by imitators in England such as Shaw, Galsworthy and Granville-Barker.

The use of asides is associated in particular with conventionalized French intrigue drama. It owes its origin to comedy, and has been handed down as a useful means of exposition from classical times, being in turn adopted by Italian, Spanish and English authors. Molière and Holberg have exploited its effects in modern times perhaps more than any comic dramatists of repute. The function of the aside is to throw light on a situation or to reveal any motive or intentions which may be obscure to the audience. It is essentially a secret between the actor and the audience, and is understood not to be heard by the other characters on the stage.

Asides were an unknown thing in tragedy. But the *bourgeois* drama of the eighteenth century revelled in them. This element of comic machinery had clung to the sentimental comedies of Steele, and, as this form of play gradually evolved into the *bourgeois* tragedy, the aside still remained as an essential feature. The first famous *bourgeois* tragedy, Lillo's *London Merchant*, has no less than twenty-three asides. With the standardization of the *drame* in France the aside became incorporated into the technique of the stage in tragedy as well as comedy. The intrigue drama of the nineteenth century, in the hands of its great exponent Eugène Scribe, adopted the aside as a technical

102

convention. The first reaction against the artificiality of the aside came from Dumas fils, who claimed by its suppression in *La Dame aux Camélias, Diane de Lys,* and *Le Demi-Monde* to have attained a greater illusion of reality. Gottsched and, later, Lessing as early as 1750 demanded a realistic motivation for the aside (*Beitr. zur Hist. und Aufnahme des Theaters*) and the German *bourgeois* dramatists Kotzebue and Iffland were in fact the first European dramatists to moderate their use of it. Hebbel, though he uses it rarely, never abandons it altogether.

Ibsen's early works reveal a complete dependence on the traditional Scribe technique in the use of asides. His first two works *Catilina* and *The Warrior's Barrow,* and the fragmentary two acts of *The Ptarmigan of Justedal,* do not however contain in all more than five asides, whereas in his short political satire *Norma,* one of the four asides is introduced with a note for special comic effect. It was only after his contact with the practical theatre that Ibsen realized the stage effectiveness of the aside. On his European study tour in 1852 he wrote a comedy, *Midsummer Eve,* which has no less than some twenty-five asides. His next play, *Lady Inger of Østråt,* contained more than twice that number (fifty-nine), and there are few things which show so strikingly Ibsen's advance in realistic technique as the revised edition of that play in 1874 in which the number of asides were reduced to five in all. The same was the case with the play that followed, *The Feast at Solhaug.* In the original version this short play contained twenty-one asides which were all excluded in the revised edition of 1883. The next play, *Olaf Liljekrans,* written in 1856, is the last play to contain asides, in the stage directions. *The Warriors of Helgeland,* written in the following year, inaugurates the complete elimination of asides from Ibsen's work. After Brandes had criticized the nature of the dialogue in *The Pretenders* and Ibsen had revised the play with particular attention to realistic illusion, he wrote to Brandes (June 26th, 1869) speaking of the corrections he had made and thanking him for his criticism. He referred to work on a play in hand (*The League of Youth*) which he said 'is written in prose and as a consequence has a strongly realistic colouring. I have treated the form with care and amongst other things have succeeded in the achievement of managing to do without a single monologue, yes, even without a single aside'. These remarks have led many people to date Ibsen's so-called realistic technique from this play. As far as monologues and asides are concerned we see, however, that they were reduced and eliminated much earlier. But while the stage direction aside disappears from the text, we find its function being substituted by stage whispers and thinking aloud. Stage whispers are an advance in objectivity because they no longer permit the character to act as a direct mouthpiece of the author. The aside breaks the continuity of the drama by reason of its undramatic nature as a commentary or explanation of the action by the author. The stage whisper, on the other hand, is realistically motivated. The characters continue the action by whispering to one another, not by confiding in the audience, with the intention that the audience shall hear what they are saying, while they appear to be speaking so that other characters on the stage shall not overhear them. Thinking aloud is merely a formally realistic development of the aside. It differs from the monologue in that the character is not alone on the stage and from the aside in that the character appears to talk to himself and does not address his remarks direct to the audience. With Ibsen it becomes even more realistic in later plays, when it is overheard by another character and is used for the development of the dialogue.

The way in which the stage whisper and thinking aloud replaced the aside may be seen by comparing the original and the revised versions of *Lady Inger of Østråt* and *The Feast at Solhaug*. In the 1857 edition of *Lady Inger* there are fifty-nine asides. In the 1874 edition there are only five. Twenty-three asides were completely suppressed, but seventeen were formally replaced by stage whispers, and fourteen by thinking aloud. In the 1855 edition of *The Feast at Solhaug* there were twenty-one asides. In the 1883 edition there were none. Two were suppressed completely, thirteen were replaced by whispers and six replaced by thinking aloud.

Effective illustrations of Ibsen's development with regard to the aside may be found in comparing plays of two different periods. In *Olaf Liljekrans*, which was written in 1856, we can find a snatch of dialogue such as the following: Olaf and Ingeborg meet in the mountains. They have run away from one another and a search party is heard approaching. Each is convinced that the other is in command of the search party which is hunting for them.

INGEBORG (*aside*) He must have ridden ahead.

OLAF (*aside*) She must have come up here with her father to search for me.

INGEBORG (*aside*) But I will not go with him.
OLAF (*aside*) I refuse to move from here.

At the beginning of the third act of *Ghosts*, when everyone is returning home after the fire, Mrs. Alving, Regine and Manders are followed by Engstrand.

REGINE (*asks*) What's the matter?
ENGSTRAND Oh, it all came of that there prayer meeting, you see. (*in a low voice*) Now, my child, we've got the fellow! (*aloud*) And to think that it should be my fault that a thing like this should be Pastor Manders' doing!

In this case Engstrand is revealing his duplicity to the audience, not by addressing them a direct aside, but by preserving the illusion and whispering to his daughter. Here we see plainly how the conventional aside underwent with Ibsen a transformation so as to conform to the scheme for producing the illusion of the fourth wall.

The stage whisper itself undergoes many transformations as Ibsen becomes a progressively more versatile technician of the stage. It is used to increase the illusion of space on the stage which becomes characteristic from the writing of *A Doll's House* onwards. This is the first of Ibsen's plays in which we have a sense of the architectural plan of the house in which the play is performed, and this is due to the dialogue rather than to the setting or stage directions. The architectural plan is filled out by characters speaking off stage, before they enter, by references to other rooms while on the stage, by talking on stage to persons off stage and by whispering on stage so that persons off stage shall not hear. The garret in *The Wild Duck* is only revealed to the audience once during the performance, but allusions to its nature and contents produce a complete illusion of reality. We never see the mill-race or the bridge in *Rosmersholm*, but we know exactly where they are.

Ibsen adapted to his own ends the clap-trap settings of romantic melodrama with its trap-doors and secret passages, and with him this eerie atmosphere of locality was assisted with asides and stage whispers.

Hedda Gabler opens with a scene between Miss Tesman and the maid Berte, who both speak in whispers, thereby creating a feeling of suspense and indicating the imminent proximity of Hedda and

Tesman. Likewise in *The Wild Duck* Gina speaks to Hedvig in a low voice so that old Ekdal shall not hear in the room next door. *The Master Builder* begins with an exchange of whispers indicative of the approach of Solness himself on the scene. There are endless instances of the realistic stage whisper to create suspense and a sense of space, beginning with *A Doll's House* and continuing to the end of Ibsen's work.

In order to avoid the improbable use of whispers on a restricted stage, Ibsen enlarges the stage, very frequently with the help of an inner room, and parades his characters backwards and forwards, leaving them on the fore-stage for opportunity to talk aloud of subjects which persons on the inner stage must not hear. When a person from the inner stage approaches them they react by changing the subject of conversation, not by a melodramatically whispered warning. In *Hedda Gabler* we have excellent instances of this. Hedda is seated on the fore-stage with Løvborg, exchanging reminiscences under the pretext of showing him photographs of her honeymoon tour. Whenever Tesman comes in from the inner room, where he is seated with Brack, she changes the subject of conversation without any intervening whisper and continues speaking in the same tone about the photographs. In the last act there is a similar scene. Tesman and Thea Elvsted are together at one side of the room piecing together Løvborg's work, while Brack at the other side of the room is blackmailing Hedda. In this case they converse aloud, but begin and conclude their conversation in whispers.

Ibsen also develops the stage whisper to complete realism, that is the whisper which is neither heard by characters on the stage nor by the audience. This again loads the atmosphere with suspense though it is a matter for the actor to give it its full dramatic significance.

In *Rosmersholm* Rebekka is talking to Rosmer, and Madam Helseth asks to speak to her. Rebekka asks her to wait, but she insists on a few words. Then the directions are as follows: 'Rebekka goes to the door. Madam Helseth gives her a message. They whisper together. Madam Helseth gives a nod and goes out.' Rosmer then asks agitatedly, 'Was it anything for me?' Rebekka replies, 'No, it was only about household matters. Now you ought to go and take a walk in the fresh air, Rosmer. You ought to take a really long walk.' Only after a long conversation does he finally go. When he has gone out Rebekka calls for Madam Helseth and Rektor Kroll is shown in.

Another form of realistic whisper used by Ibsen is a development of the dumb-show whisper. It is the whisper which is inaudible to the audience but which is communicated to them by the audible reply of the person to whom it is addressed. Thus in *The Wild Duck* we read the following: Hedvig (puts her arm round Hjalmar's neck and whispers in his ear). Hjalmar. 'No. No bread and butter now.' This type of whisper does not recur often in Ibsen's plays. It has been adopted by later dramatists for telephone conversations.

These are the variations which the aside undergoes in its contribution to the realistic illusion of Ibsen's plays. It disappeared in its most primitive form in 1857 with *The Warriors of Helgeland*, the first play in which he used the technique of retrospective exposition. It was probably the adoption of this type of exposition which permitted a descriptive treatment of plot and character that made the omission of the aside possible, but it was above all Ibsen's insistence on the illusion of realism that made the exclusion of the aside a matter of technical principle.

The monologue in its most primitive form was used both in tragedy and comedy as a convenient means for narrative exposition. Its function was such in the Greek and Roman theatre, in the mystery and morality plays and in the popular Italian farces. The Renaissance extends its function. Shakespeare and Racine both use the reflective monologue to help the action in the course of the play. The French classical dramatists were advised by d'Aubignac to avoid the monologue exposition and to divide the task between one of the protagonists and his confidant. In the sentimental *bourgeois* drama of the eighteenth century we find the same state of affairs as with the aside. The plays bear marks of their double origin. In comedy the narrative monologue remained as a legitimate device long after it had been abandoned in tragedy, and, as such, it was transferred to the *bourgeois* drama, becoming in fact a sort of lengthy aside. The reflective monologue was also incorporated with *bourgeois* tragedy; but as psychology gradually becomes subordinate to intrigue the monologue loses its function, and either is shortened to the length of one exclamation or is developed merely into a tirade of sentimental emotion. Moore's play, *The Gamester*, which ranks high among plays of this type, gives admir-

107

able instances of the standardization of the monologue into the two types, the narrative and explanatory on the one side and the emotional on the other. Stukely, the villain, when unable to reveal his evil machinations to the audience with the aid of asides, uses the explanatory monologue to help the intrigue. Beverley, the victim, on the other hand, regularly gives vent to his emotion in monologues of self-reproach, especially before his suicide and prolonged death at the end of the play. These two types of monologue were adopted by the intrigue dramatists of the nineteenth century, and only after coming into intimate touch with their work did Ibsen realize the effectiveness of the explanatory monologue on the stage.

The monologues in *Catilina* are reflective and stand under the influence of Shakespeare, Schiller and Oehlenschlæger. Only after his European tour in 1852 do we find in Ibsen's comedy, *Midsummer Eve*, the first instances of using the monologue as an aid to exposition. The first monologue of this type in Ibsen's work is spoken by Mrs. Berg at the end of the first scene of the latter play (*Eft. Skr*. I. 375), when she reveals the fact that there are some important papers to be found and concludes with the words: 'I must find out for certain, I cannot rest until I have done so.'

The same is the case with *Lady Inger* and *Olaf Liljekrans*. The latter play contains the last full-length 'aside' monologue in Ibsen's work (*Saml. Vaerker*, 1902, Vol. X, p. 157). In this monologue Olaf informs the audience that Alfhild is the daughter of Ingrid, who eloped many years ago with a wandering musician Thorgjerd. This dispels the illusion that she is a fairy and prepares the way for his betrothal to her at the end of the play.

With *The Warriors of Helgeland* we meet with a new technique, as in the case of the aside. The explanatory monologue is abandoned, the monologue is reduced in length to a few words, finally taking the form of epigrammatic generalities to round off an act, and, but for the fact that it is spoken with the character alone on the stage, it is identical with what has earlier been defined as 'thinking aloud'. (In the illustrative table the monologue and 'thinkings aloud' recorded in brackets are those which can scarcely be distinguished from one another. They have been recorded as identical on the graphs.) The only plays after *The Warriors of Helgeland* to use conventional monologues were *The Pretenders* and the two epic verse dramas, *Brand* and *Peer Gynt*. Ibsen consciously eliminated both monologues and thinking aloud from *The League of Youth*, but there are only two plays written afterwards which eliminate both of these devices completely (*An Enemy of the People* and *Little Eyolf*), and it seems that Ibsen never made up his mind completely on this point. He is consistent in curtailing the length of the monologue, but sure enough, both explanatory and reflective monologues recur in his later plays, as may be seen from the figures in the illustrative table.

The second act of *A Doll's House*, for instance, begins with the charming monologue which so penetratingly reveals Nora's state of mind and her naïve nature, ending with the words: 'Oh, nonsense. Of course he won't take it seriously. Nothing of the kind could possibly happen. It is impossible. I've got three small children.' And when the blackmailer Krogstad leaves her, Nora peeps through the door leading to the hall and in an explanatory monologue describes to the audience how he drops the incriminating letter in the box. A similar descriptive monologue appears in *Rosmersholm* at the end, when Rosmer and Rebekka have left to commit suicide in the mill-race and Madam Helseth stands at the window talking to herself as she watches them go. But it must be remembered that this type of monologue is not an intrigue device; it is not used to unravel a complicated situation, but like the messenger of classical tragedy has the function of describing action which it is not convenient to present on the stage.

It seems that Ibsen realized that the abolition of the monologue was just as artificial as the abolition of verse in his later plays. He accepted it as a legitimate device and modified it to fit his scheme of realistic illusion, but he never cast it aside altogether. Strindberg reinstated the monologue for the very reason that almost made Ibsen abandon it, namely realistic motivation, and it must be conceded that the realistic illusion of his one act play *The Stronger* is in no way impaired by the fact that the whole play is one long monologue. Ibsen, however, was too submissive to the conventions of his own technique to launch out on such experiments.

STATISTICAL TABLE OF ASIDES, STAGE WHISPERS, MONOLOGUES AND
THINKING ALOUD IN IBSEN'S PLAYS

Play	Asides	Stage whispers	Mono-logues	Thinking aloud
Catilina	1	2	11	7
The Warrior's Barrow	3	0	3	0
The Ptarmigan of Justedal	2	0	4	0
Midsummer Eve	25	13	7	4
Lady Inger of Østråt {	59 (1857 ed.) 5 (1874 ed.)	26	11	21
The Feast at Solhaug {	21 (1856 ed.) 0 (1883 ed.)	24	5	9
Olaf Liljekrans	34	20	6	8
The Warriors of Helgeland	0	13	(3)	2
Love's Comedy	0	8	0	2
The Pretenders	0	18	5	(3)
Brand	0	11	14	7
Peer Gynt	0	8	25	1
The League of Youth	0	14	0	0
Emperor and Galilean I	0	29	0	1
II	0	7	0	1
The Pillars of Society	0	13	0	1
A Doll's House	0	7	(7)	0
Ghosts	0	4	(4)	0
An Enemy of the People	0	6	0	0
The Wild Duck	0	9	0	2
Rosmersholm	0	(1)	(2)	0
The Lady from the Sea	0	8	(2)	0
Hedda Gabler	0	(17)	(3)	0
The Master Builder	0	9	(1)	0
Little Eyolf	0	7	0	0
J. G. Borkman	0	3	(6)	0
When We Dead Awaken	0	4	(3)	0

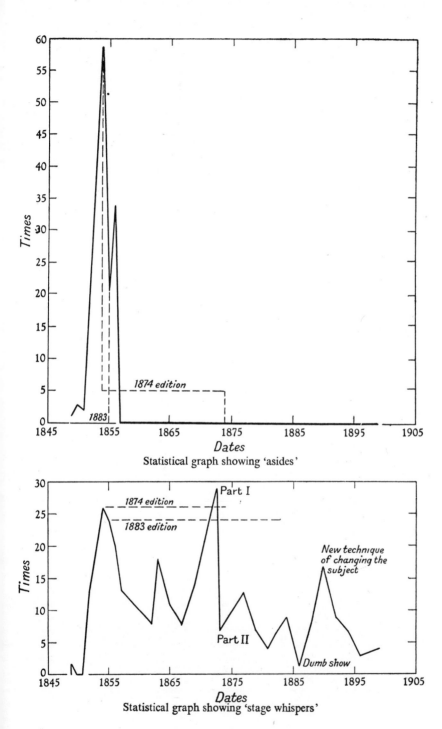

Statistical graph showing 'asides'

Statistical graph showing 'stage whispers'

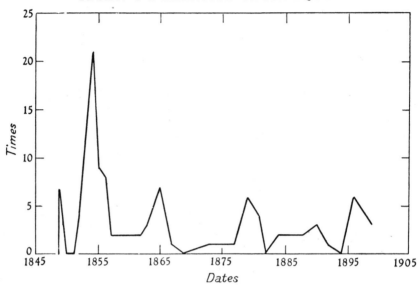

Statistical graph showing 'monologues'

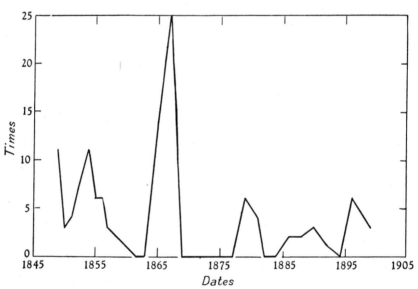

Statistical graph showing 'thinking aloud'

112

CHAPTER VII

THE ENDING

ONE of the distinctions between tragedy and comedy was the traditional difference between the happy and sad endings. Originally these endings could be brought about quite arbitrarily by the intervention of a deity or some fortuitous coincidence. Aristotle, however, advocated in tragedy the logical *dénouement* which was brought about by the characters themselves, and he was followed by the pseudo-classical dramatists and theorists of the Renaissance, who used a seemingly inexorable logic to bring about the catastrophe. But the *Deus ex machinâ* remained a favourite device in comedy and tragi-comedy and this became true of the sentimental domestic drama of the eighteenth century. This drama was the product of a conscious mixture of tragedy and comedy, and formed the basis for the developments of social drama in the nineteenth century. Its conciliatory endings were a sop cast to the sentimental taste of the day, and we find this idea of reconciliation dominating German neo-classic drama (*Iphigenie, Die Jungfrau von Orleans*) and pre-eminent among romantic dramatists. Hebbel was the first dramatist to make a theoretical onslaught against this conception, and his dramas themselves are pervaded by a sense of logical inevitability. But even Hebbel allows a compromise, for, whereas the individual in most cases succumbs to the force of circumstances, the dramatic conflict is usually resolved with Hegelian speciousness by a suggestion of synthesis and the triumph of the idea. But Hebbel during his lifetime was of no importance for the European theatre, and the old traditions of the happy ending at any price were continued by the most popular dramatists of the period, Dumas fils and Augier.

When Ibsen began to write it was only natural that he should adopt the traditional endings of the contemporary stage. He was a young man making his name, and nothing is inclined to meet with such disfavour with an audience as sending them home displeased or disconcerted by an unconventional ending. His endings only became typical of his technique when he could afford to make them so with *A Doll's House*. Up till the publication of the latter play we meet with only conventional endings. The modern plays that precede *A Doll's House* are partly for this very reason the least characteristic of all his work. *The League of Youth* and *Pillars of Society* are much more like the work of Augier or Freytag than of Ibsen. Both these plays have conciliatory endings. In *The League of Youth* Steensgård is punished, Erik Brattsberg is converted, there are two reconciliations (The Chamberlain with Erik, and Selma with Erik) and three betrothals. *Pillars of Society* follows the same formula of punishment, conversion and reconciliation. *The Enemy of the People*, which was written in 1882, is the only other comedy of Ibsen's later period, but although the play, which almost borders on tragedy, ends on a note of optimism there is none of the traditional battery of effects in the *dénouement*.

In his earlier plays Ibsen conformed to the accepted conventions in romantic historical drama and the classical tragedy of Goethe and Schiller. His first play *Catilina* ends with the death of the hero and his wife, but the traditional note of harmony is introduced by a sunrise at the end, an effect which Ibsen repeats so melodramatically in *Ghosts*. A symbol of harmony and reconciliation is incorporated into the endings of nearly all his early plays, if not in the dialogue or action, then in a tableau or stage effect. His romantic vaudeville plays (*Midsummer Eve, The Feast at Solhaug, Olaf Liljekrans*) conform to the formulae laid down for this type of drama by the Dane, J. L. Heiberg, and practised by playwrights in Norway, Denmark and Sweden from the 1830s to the 1860s, when the national romantic genre was so successfully parodied by Skavlan. Here Ibsen, after a series of discoveries, misunderstandings and recognitions, ends with the punishment of the villain and a succession of betrothals and reconciliations.

Not until *Brand* and *Love's Comedy* do we meet with any signs of reaction. The *dénouement* of *Brand* is in full accordance with the uncompromising tendencies of the play, and the rabid idealist is swept away in an avalanche; but a concession is made to the audience, as in the case of Goethe's *Faust*, and Brand's soul is saved, like Gretchen's, with the voice which answers his appeal to God, 'He is *deus caritatis*'. In *Love's Comedy* Ibsen has delighted, like Becque, in satirizing the conventions of drawing-room comedy. Just as Becque in *Les corbeaux* lets the first act end with a death and the last act with an unhappy betrothal and leaves us at the end of the play as unhappy as when we began, so Ibsen lets the two lovers Falk and Svanhild break off their engagement, and Svanhild, against all the rules for the triumph of young love, becomes engaged for purely material reasons to the rich business man, Guldstad.

One type of romatic tragedy however was all-important in Ibsen's adoption of the uncompromisingly tragic ending; this was the romantic fate-tragedy. The conception of fate is based on an illusion of logic and is in strong contrast to the drama of chance and situation, though in combination with these latter elements the coincidences become more convincing, since they appear to obey the unseen hand of destiny. Fate-tragedy represented a crude revival of the Greek idea of fate, but instead of being based on firm religious convictions it was founded on a passion for sensation and superstition, typical of that romantic egotism which was fond of seeing divine or supernatural intervention in human affairs. The conception is based on faulty logic, a *post hoc non propter*, which tries to associate a series of coincidences by a chain of cause and effect where no causal sequence can in fact be demonstrated. This faulty logic is supported by the nonconformist conscience, with its conception of guilt and sin and the inevitable retribution that follows. This is in fact the simple moral basis of all Ibsen's tragedies. A character has sinned and events combine to bring about retribution. One of his earliest plays, *Lady Inger*, is practically a full-blooded fate-tragedy, and the conventional apparatus of fate-tragedy can be traced even in his later plays as a device for bringing about the catastrophe. *Ghosts* has already been mentioned, but an even later play, *The Wild Duck*, has traces of the outward mechanism remaining in the shape of the fatal pistol with which Hjalmar and his father have almost committed suicide and with which Hedvig finally does kill herself. The fact that the play begins with a dinner-party with thirteen guests at table is also significant. Similarly the pistols in *Hedda Gabler* are a survival of the traditional fatal objects, and the white horses which haunt *Rosmersholm* help to give the suicide of Rosmer and Rebekka in the fatal mill-race an illusion of inevitability. The whole family background of Ibsen's plays tends to approximate to the themes of fate-tragedy with its purely family conflicts between parents and children, brothers and sisters, and themes such as illegitimacy and incest, the latter of which plays such a prominent part in *Ghosts, Rosmersholm*, and *Little Eyolf*.

The fate which dominates Ibsen's tragedies creates the

115

catastrophe in the form of death, which usually takes the shape of suicide. There are exceptions, however, and in these plays the characters succeed in asserting themselves against fate. Nora takes her destiny into her own hands in *A Doll's House* and walks out of the house to start life over again. In *The Lady from the Sea* the heroine Ellida believes she is fatally bewitched by the mysterious stranger, but her husband plays the part of the psycho-analyst and frees her from her obsession. In *Little Eyolf* the catastrophe occurs in the first act; Rita and Allmers are punished for their sensuality by the death of their crippled son Eyolf, but instead of committing suicide they sustain two more acts and finally sublimate their fatal desires by finding a common interest in starting a home for waifs and strays. But in all Ibsen's other tragedies death is the accepted ending, and death takes the form of a responsible action, suicide, or at least something approaching it. This is in strong contrast to the convenient murders or duels of situation drama, where death is brought about not by the characters but by an outside agent. Murder is with Ibsen rarely a solution, and occurs only in *The Feast at Solhaug*, *The Warriors of Helgeland*, and *The Pretenders*. Otherwise Ibsen's heroes die what one might call responsible deaths, from Catiline who is a victim of a bad con- science to Rubek and Irene in *When We Dead Awaken*, who flaunt the elements like Brand and die a romantic *Liebestod* in an avalanche.

There is, however, yet another element in Ibsen's endings, their frequent inconclusiveness. This is partly a survival of romantic optimism, which nourished a predeliction for heroes dying in the rays of the rising sun, heralding in a new and better age. It is partly a technical device to preserve the dramatic suspense until the very end and partly an effect based on a conception of life which Ibsen considered more true than that represented by the stage convention of a conclusively happy or tragic end as the curtain falls. The inconclusive ending he first introduced with *A Doll's House* and it was this that led to so many protests, adaptations and sequel stories when the play first appeared. In Germany Frau Raabe refused to act the part of Nora unless a happy ending were introduced, protesting with the words: 'I would never leave my children.' A happy ending had to be substituted in Germany. In one version Nora hears the cries of her children and, like a Dumas heroine, heeds the call of duty and remains, collapsing at the entrance to the nursery. In another version another act was added. Here Nora is seen with a new-born child on her lap sitting with Mrs. Linde who is now married to Krogstad and happy. Helmer comes in, steals up behind Nora, puts his hands over her eyes, takes a bag of the forbidden maca-roons out of his pocket and pops one in Nora's mouth. She then exclaims: 'The miracle has happened,' and the curtain falls slowly to the accompaniment of tender embraces. When Henry Arthur Jones and Henry Herman adapted the play in England in 1884 they gave the play a happy ending and changed the title to the sentimental *Breaking a Butterfly.* Ibsen's ending to the play was considered of supreme importance, because here for the first time the family as a social institution was attacked on the stage in a form of drama which had previously owed its popularity to the support which it had given to family life and the sacred conventions of marriage and filial piety. It was however not only the attack on social conditions but also the inconclusiveness of the play that worried Ibsen's contemporaries. People wanted to know what happened afterwards. Ibsen met the same question with *Ghosts.* Did Mrs. Alving give her son the fatal dose of morphia or not? He told W. Archer that he had not considered the matter. Such .questions were beside the point, and from an examination of Ibsen's composition of *A Doll's House* it is clear that he had a purpose in introducing this element of inconclusiveness in his *dénouements.*

During the winter of 1878-1879 in Rome, while he was writing *A Doll's House,* his chief companion was the Danish writer J. P. Jacobsen, the first Scandinavian translator of Darwin's works. Darwinism originally occupied a very large portion of the play, and these themes reflect the conversations Ibsen had with Jacobsen on the subject. While, however, the great majority of the discussions on heredity, natural selection and the effect of environment were omitted from the final draft, it seems that the ending itself had been conceived with reference to the theories of evolution. Just after the storm about *A Doll's House* had broken out Jacobsen remarks in one of his letters (March 14th, 1880) on the idiotic convention of a happy ending as being against nature, and writes : 'The only possible ending is death, or else, since human relation-ships are eternally inconclusive, one should finish a work with an indication of further continuation as Ibsen does in *A Doll's House.*'

A noticeable resemblance to these remarks is found in the words of Dr. Rank, the first Darwinistic *raisonneur* of Ibsen's plays, when he speaks in Act II of death and says that life will continue afterwards 'making new relationships' and forgetting the dead. A fortnight later (March 30th, 1880) Jacobsen takes up the question again. 'It has lately become the fashion among scientists', he writes, 'to say that too much stress has been laid on the question of evolution. This accusation cannot with justification be flung at "works of fiction". Because here it is nearly always a question of completed states; even when attempts are made at it, it is never real evolution, it is only a certain fixed form, which page after page is even more richly shaded, more and more stressed. It never has the possibility in it of all possibilities by which it gains in solidarity but not in life.' Now Ibsen was already used to ending his plays with a question mark. His sudden shirking of responsibility at the end of *Brand* made readers, who were sure of Brand's fate in this world, ask what his chances were of redemption in the next. Ibsen himself wrote: 'I prefer to ask, it is not my task to answer.' It seems that Darwinism gave fresh stimulus to his questioning, and while it gave new force to his fatalism, he may have adopted the inconclusive ending as a definite technical device which possibly owed its origin to discussions with Jacobsen.

Ibsen's use of realism was closely tied to romantic symbolism, with its desire for classical harmony, which in the greatest catastrophe can see a triumph of the personality. In spite of the gloomy prospect of life continuing as before, there is a note of optimism when the rising sun shines on Osvald's death; Rosmer and Rebekka attain their ideals of nobility when they throw themselves into the mill-race; Hedda Gabler's suicide is her liberation, and Solness's fall makes of him the ideal figure of which Hilde had dreamed. Ibsen's endings show only too clearly how his efforts to create a realistic illusion were tempered by the use of romantic symbolism.

CHAPTER VIII

CONCLUSION

IBSEN's method of exposition, his treatment of the stage, were of infinite importance for the dramatists who followed him, because he in some cases broke with, in others developed, the conventional manner of French drawing-room drama. There are many other sides of Ibsen's dramatic technique which might have been considered here. His characters and his method of characterization are an example; but in this particular field Ibsen contributed little to the history of drama. The majority of his characters, except for some tragic heroines, are types constructed for the demonstration of a moral principle. Ibsen usually brings home his sympathies and antipathies among his characters by making his men into caricatures of hypocritical clergymen, journalists, politicians, lawyers, officials, merchants and public men, against whom he sets off their tragic female victims, who are usually endowed with the most human qualities among his gallery of personalities. Even many of these women are strikingly bloodless, and it is interesting to see how Ibsen's only great psychological studies are to be found in plays where the moralistic element is lacking, with such characters as Hjalmar Ekdal in *The Wild Duck*, Rebekka West in *Rosmersholm*, and Hedda Gabler. His Brand and his Peer Gynt are two great poetic figures which cannot be measured by the standards of his later social dramas. The great majority of his characters are, however, mere ciphers whose behaviour is conditioned by the structure of the play, and the social and moral problems which form the dramatic situations with which they are in conflict.

Another omission is perhaps the question of style, and Ibsen's treatment of dramatic dialogue. Ibsen aimed at the difficult task of echoing everyday language in his social plays, but his great contribution to the Norwegian language is undoubtedly to be found in his verse, above all in his poetic plays, *Brand* and *Peer Gynt*; but the discussion of Ibsen's verse does not come within the scope of this study. Ibsen's treatment of prose dialogue, though conversational, is strikingly lacking in variation. Nearly all of his characters speak the same language, and Hjalmar Ekdal is one of

119

the few whom he succeeds in characterizing by individual turns of speech. As far as the dialogue affects the dramatic structure it has been referred to already.

Ibsen, as a dramatist, is neither primarily a thinker nor a psychologist; he is an illusionist and artist, and as such, his contribution to the theatre is a lasting one. The illusion is brought home by the apparent moral sincerity behind it. Ibsen's moral indignation could slur over many psychological weaknesses and his dramatic technique was able to create illusion by freely using the borrowed trappings of contemporary thought. John Stuart Mill's utilitarianism, Kierkegaard's rectitudinitis, the Darwinist jargon of heredity, natural selection and the influence of environment, combined with Old Testament and Lutheran doctrines of sin and retribution, produce in the nonconformist conscience of the strait-laced Ibsen an honest conviction of morality being synonymous with happiness, of truth and individual freedom being the greatest good, and of divine wrath visiting punishment in the form of disease, degeneration or a sickly conscience on all those, who for material interests, fail to follow the path of righteousness and the vocation to which they have been called. This highly romantic ideal is given an illusion of stark reality by the dramatic technique with which it is presented. It is this technique of Ibsen's which deluded his contemporaries into accepting him as a thinker. It is the same technique which for posterity has marked him as a dramatist of the first order.

In his day he was looked upon as a moralist and a preacher, to the utter extinction of his art. But Ibsen never failed to disclaim association with the gospels preached by his characters, and he wrote his plays as dialectical contradictions. Brand, the idealist, with his all-or-nothing principles, was followed by the opportunist Peer Gynt, who made his way in the world by always avoiding the issue. Like many Norwegians and Danes, Ibsen was plagued with a Janus-like personality. Like Holberg and Kierkegaard, he had a faculty for seeing two sides of a question, but innate moral cowardice forbade him ever to take sides. He was both Brand and Peer Gynt in one person, but disclaimed responsibility for both of them. He sets up ideals in *Pillars of Society*, in *Ghosts*, in *A Doll's House* and in *The Enemy of the People*, and coins a jargon about truth, the realization of personality, and the claims of the individual, which are knocked down like skittles by the caricature of the ideal-monger Gregers Werle in *The Wild Duck*. The true marriage, loyalty to one's vocation, the right to free choice and the doom of past misdeeds recur in varying forms as *leitmotifs* in all his modern social dramas, but suddenly misgivings take hold of him, and he begins, with *The Master Builder*, to look back on his own life. The last series of confessional plays pronounce perhaps the most honest and damning judgment that has ever been made on an artist by himself. Ibsen, looking back on life in *When We Dead Awaken*, makes Professor Rubek say: 'I was only an artist.' This was Ibsen's final judgment on himself, on the little old man who buttoned himself out of contact with the world in the folds of an ample frock-coat, who lay in wait and spied on his fellow-beings, without daring to share their lives.

Strindberg, in an antagonistic moment, wrote of Ibsen (May 4th, 1884) to Bjørnson: 'You know, I am beginning to feel a sneaking dislike for Ibsen after *The Enemy of the People*. There is something unreliably aesthetic about him. Writing *Brand* with the Medschidi order round his neck.' (He received this at the opening of the Suez Canal, in fact, some years later.) 'And the *Doll's House*! Ibsen, the old misogynist! It was a move that had the great merit of coming off! When Fru Hvasser wrote and asked him what he meant by the play, and if Nora was to return, he answered that he didn't know! There you have the aesthete and medal-hunter!' Strindberg was the only contemporary who sensed Ibsen's failure to live up to the principles enunciated by his characters, and it needed a man with the nervous sensitiveness of Strindberg to feel the disparity to the full. Ibsen himself felt it, however, and a realization of this dualism between art and life forms the main theme of the last plays, beginning with *The Master Builder*.

Once, when entertained at a society of emancipated women at Stockholm, he said he did not know what emancipation was. He read Mill's *Subjection of Woman* and hated it, though he incorporated much of the argument, lock, stock and barrel, into his plays. From his earliest youth, however, he was an aesthete, in spite of the apparent contact with life he makes through the characters of his plays. He found a refuge in Art from the painful experiences of his childhood and youth, and in his early poem 'On the Heights' he symbolizes an attitude to life which he retains to the end of his days. He stands on the heights looking with complete detachment on the burning of his family home and the marriage of the woman he had loved, shading his eyes with the hollow of his hand to enhance the effect of perspective.

When he wrote *Brand*, all indications point to the fact that he identified himself with the character while writing, though he disclaimed all connection afterwards. A young Norwegian lady, later known to us as Laura Kieler, wrote a sequel to the play entitled *Brand's Daughters* and sent it to Ibsen for criticism. Ibsen liked the style but regretted her evangelical zeal, and said: '*Brand* was an aesthetic work, not a shadow of anything else.' Later he exploited the story of this young lady's early married life in the theme of *A Doll's House*. She immediately broke off her friendly relations with the Ibsens for this breach of discretion. Her story was well known, and the literary success of *A Doll's House* made her position intolerable in Copenhagen society. Ibsen was begged to alleviate her distress by publicly denying that he had taken Laura Kieler as a model for Nora. He shilly-shallied and avoided the issue by saying that it was her husband's business and not his to defend her reputation. Later, in 1891, twelve years after the play was written, she visited him in Oslo. They sat for four hours and discussed the position. She took him back to *Brand* and his letter in which he disclaimed responsibility for the ideals of the play. She reproached him with moral cowardice, and in the words of Brand himself demanded that Ibsen should do what he could to save her reputation. Old Min wept. It is the only recorded occasion on which he melted in public. 'It is impossible,' he said, and begged her to go away. She went, and they never met again. But that year appeared *The Master Builder* and, like Laura Kieler, Hilde Wangel comes to Solness and demands that he shall fulfil the promises made to her. Solness, like Ibsen, has won fame at the expense of human happiness. As Ibsen had written his religious play *Brand* without living up to its principles, and then reverted to the problems of everyday life, so also Solness had first built churches and then started to build homes for human beings because he was unable to climb the steeples. Now his evil conscience makes him build a tower which he will climb for the delight of his admirer. So also Ibsen makes a final bid for life, but, as an inborn aesthete, fails. In the same way John Gabriel Borkman leaves his prison to walk out in the winter snow and die in contact with reality. So also the sculptor Rubek, taking his old love Irene with him, leaves his art and the memories of his past, and they climb the hills in a last effort to live again, but are overwhelmed, like Brand, by an avalanche and killed.

It was thus that the old Ibsen looked back on his life, the life of the artist who escaped the responsibilities of reality by projecting reality into his work and keeping it at arm's length. Now that the superstructure of topical problems is no longer of much consequence to us to-day, it is easier to see how superfluous these problems are and how permanent is the artistic value of Ibsen's work. His aesthetic detachment as a poet, however it may have exasperated Strindberg or the poor individuals who suffered as his models, seems to be the very quality in Ibsen's nature which has saved his work from the fate of passing into oblivion with his time.

CHRONOLOGY OF IBSEN'S LIFE AND WORKS

early works

1828   *Ibsen born,* March 20th, in Skien, Norway. Eldest son of a family of five, four sons and one daughter. Father, Knud Ibsen, a business man. Mother, Marichen Altenburg, of German stock.

1836   The Ibsens move out of the town to farm at Venstøp after Knud Ibsen's bankruptcy.

1843   *October 1st,* Ibsen confirmed. The family returns to Skien and Ibsen leaves for Grimstad.

1844   Apothecary's apprentice in Grimstad. Earns his own living henceforward for the rest of his life. Abjectly poor. No friends from age of 16-19.

1846   Father of illegitimate child by one of the maids in the apothecary's house. Pays maintenance for fourteen years.

1847   First surviving poem written: 'Resignation'.
Takes apothecary's examination. Better salary. Moves to better quarters. Takes lessons with young theologian Monrad. Friendship with Christopher Due and Ole Schulerud. Interest in European revolutions. Reads Kierkegaard.

1848   G. A. Lammers, sectarian preacher, comes to Skien and is followed by Ibsen's sister and brother Ole.

1849   Ibsen's social life begins.
Walks and boating trips with young people of Grimstad.
Winter, goes to his first ball.
Play, *Catilina,* written during first months of the year; planned 1848.
Patriotic poems.
Autumn. Falls in love with Clara Ebbel.
September 28th, first poem printed. Signed with pseudonym Brynjolf Bjarme.
October, first act of play, *Olav Trygveson,* finished.
One act play, *Normannerne,* finished.
Plans for a story about Christian Lofthus, 'The Prisoner of Akershus'.
Versifications of stories and legends from Telemark.

1850   Jilted by Clara Ebbel. Falls in love with another.
April 12th, Catilina printed at Ole Schulerud's expense.
April 15th, leaves Grimstad.
April 29th, arrives in Christiania.

124

Enters Heltberg's crammer. Meets A. O. Vinje, Frithiof Foss. Lived in lodgings with Schulerud. Poor.

Autumn. Publishes revised version of *Normannerne* as *The Warrior's Barrow* (*Kjæmpehøjen*). First play to be performed.

August. Takes 'artium'. Fails in Greek and mathematics. Gives up idea of career as doctor. Takes part in student life. Literary interests. Writes poetry.

The Ptarmigan in Justedal (*Rypen i Justedal*) written. A romantic comedy of which only two acts remain.

1851 Journalism. Edits student paper. Writes for Abildgaard's workers' paper.

July. 7 leaders of workers' union arrested, including Abildgaard. Becomes joint editor of satirical paper *Andhrimmer* with A. O. Vinje and Botten-Hansen. Publishes anonymously short political parody of Bellim's opera *Norma* in *Andhrimmer* June 1st to 8th.

The Dane, Carl Borgaard, becomes manager of Christiania Theatre.

Publishes lyrics for the Scandinavian students' meeting in Christiania, for the first time signing his own name.

Ole Bull takes Ibsen to Bergen, to his National Theatre.

November 6th, Ibsen signs contract to assist the theatre as dramatist with a salary of about four pounds a month for half a year. Begins by writing prologues.

1852 *February.* Bergen theatre grants Ibsen a travelling grant of about forty pounds for studying the theatre in Denmark and Germany, with a prospect of later becoming stage manager and producer.

April 15th, leaves Bergen with Johannes and Louise Brun. From Hamburg he travels to Copenhagen. Given all facilities at the Royal Theatre by the manager, J. L. Heiberg, and the stage manager, T. Overskou.

June 6th, leaves Copenhagen and arrives in Dresden on *June 9th.* Here he studied the court theatre until *September* when he returns to Bergen. Given a subordinate position in the theatre.

1853 *January 2nd,* Ibsen's play, *Midsummer Eve* (*Sancthansnatten*), written during his tour, performed to a full house. Failure.

May. Moves from Madam Sontum's hotel to two rooms in the theatre annexe. Lonely life. Excessively elegant manners and dress.

Falls in love with 15½ year old Rikke Holst.

June. Proposes to her in verse. Secret betrothal broken by Rikke's irate father.

1854   *New Year. The Warrior's Barrow (Kjæmpehøjen)*, performed once. Failure.
Writes *Lady Inger of Østråt (Fru Inger til Østråt)*.

1855   *January 2nd, Lady Inger of Østråt (Fru Inger til Østråt)* performed. Failure.
Summer. Writes *The Feast at Solhaug (Gildet på Solhaug)*.
Becomes a member of a Bergen literary society.
November 27th, reads the society a paper on 'Shakespeare and his influence on nordic art'.

1856   *January 2nd, The Feast at Solhaug (Gildet på Solhaug)* performed. Great success. Six performances.
January 7th, invited for the first time to the house of Magdalene Thoresen where he met his future wife, the 19 year old Susannah, for the first time.
March 19th, The Feast at Solhaug (Gildet på Solhaug) published in Oslo, the first play to be published after *Catilina*.
Wrote next play, *Olaf Liljekrans*.

1857   *January 2nd, Olaf Liljekrans* performed. Taken off after second night.
February 2nd, reads paper to literary society on 'The chivalrous ballad and its significance for literary poetry'.
April 1st, contract expires with Bergen theatre.
April 11th, signs contract for one more year.
Christiania Norwegian Theatre offers him double his Bergen salary. Goes to Christiania to investigate.
July 23rd, letter to Bergen theatre asking to be released from contract.
August 11th, signs contract with Christiania Norwegian Theatre.
September 3rd, becomes 'artistic manager' in Christiania. Meets Bjørnson who then goes to take over in Bergen.
Play *The Warriors of Helgeland (Hærmændene på Helgeland)* written.
November. The play is accepted by the Christiania Theatre. Due for production in spring.

1858   *February.* J. L. Heiberg refuses *The Warriors of Helgeland (Hærmændene på Helgeland)* for Danish Royal Theatre.
March 9th, hears that the Christiania Theatre has put off playing *The Warriors of Helgeland (Hærmændene på Helgeland)* for a year in view of expense.
March 10th, attacks the Christiania Theatre in *Aftenbladet*. Conflict of Norwegian and Danish theatre begins.
April. The Warriors of Helgeland (Hærmændene på Helgeland) published in *Illustreret Nyhedsblad*.

June 18*th*, marries Susannah Thoresen.
November. Ibsen produces *The Warriors of Helgeland* (*Hærmæn-dene på Helgeland*) at his own theatre.
Period of artistic inactivity begins. Creative desires satisfied by painting until 1861.

1859   *April*. *Lady Inger* produced at his theatre.
Friendship with Bjørnson who returns to Christiania as editor of *Aftenbladet*.
November. Founds the Norwegian Society with Bjørnson's help.
Writes pessimistic poem 'On the Heights', fragment of an opera *Fjeldfuglen* based on Olaf Liljekrans and play *Svanhild*.
Member of Botten-Hansen's circle 'Det lærde Holland'.
Association with Vinje, Sars, Bjørnson, Birkeland, Daae, Rygh, Bachke, Løkke. Cult of Holberg.

1860   Applies with Bjørnson and Vinje for a government stipend.
Bjørnson and Vinje granted, Ibsen refused.
Despair and melancholy, illness, thoughts of suicide, neglects work at theatre.

1861   *March-April*. Defends himself in newspapers against attacks on his theatre.
Writes poem 'Terje Vigen'. Mental and physical recovery.
Success in theatre with productions of Bjørnson's *Halte-Hulda* and *King Sverre* and with de Musset's *Un caprice*.

1862   *May*. University grant for collection of folk-songs and tales.
Summer. Norwegian Theatre bankrupt.
Rewrites *Svanhild* in verse as *Love's Comedy* (*Kjærlighedens Komedie*). Not performed. Poor reception as new year's eve supplement to *Illustreret Nyhedsblad*.

1863   *New Year*. Becomes literary adviser to Christiania Theatre.
Half a year later all the Norwegian actors from the Norwegian theatre follow him.
March 10*th*, application to Government for financial support.
Not granted. Bad finances. Resorts to money-lenders.
May 23*rd*, procures a grant from University for study tour to collect folk-songs in the country.
May 27*th*, applies for Government grant to study abroad.
Writes *The Pretenders* (*Kongs-emnerne*) living on proceeds of university grant.
July 19*th*, first biography of Ibsen published by Botten-Hansen.
September 12*th*, granted a travel stipend by the Government which was later augmented by private contributions collected by Bjørnson, Bernhard Dunker and Johan Sverdrup.

October. The Pretenders (*Kongs-emnerne*) published and accepted by Christiania Theatre.

1864   *January 17th, The Pretenders* (*Kongs-emnerne*) performed at the Christiania Theatre. Success.

April 5th, leaves Christiania for Copenhagen.

Plans for drama about Magnus Heineson.

Ibsen's fury at Schleswig-Holstein war. Anti-German bitterness over failure of Swedes and Norwegians to help Danes.

April 18th, attack on Dybbøl while Ibsen was in Copenhagen.

April 20th, Ibsen leaves Copenhagen for Lübeck and then Berlin.

May 4th, sees Danish canons paraded through Berlin. Travels to Vienna.

May 9th, crosses the Alps to Rome. Meets Scandinavians in Scandinavian Club. Moves to Genzano.

September. Returns to Rome. Joined by wife and son a few months later. Plans for a play about Julian the Apostate. Begins work on first epic version of *Brand*.

1865   *Spring.* Continues work on Julian and *Brand*.

Summer. Moves to Arricia.

Hegel of Gyldendal's publishing house in Copenhagen sends Ibsen an advance and becomes his publisher by contract.

November. Brand finished and sent to Hegel.

Plans work on Magnus Heineson drama again.

1866   *March 15th, Brand* issued in an edition of 1250 copies with two further editions the same year, and brings Ibsen success and financial security.

Spring. Work on Julian.

April 30th, voted a pecuniary grant by Trondheim Scientific Association.

May 12th, granted an annual stipend by the Norwegian Government.

June 28th, new travel grant voted by the Norwegian Government.

June-September, lived at Frascati. Revision of *Love's Comedy* (*Kjærlighedens Komedie*) for Danish public.

Reaction against Norwegian nationalism.

Christmas. First plans for *Peer Gynt*.

1867   *New Year.* Work on *Peer Gynt*.

May-July. Stays in Ischia.

August-September. Moves to Sorrento. *Peer Gynt* finished.

October. Pompeii, Naples, Rome. Witnesses Garibaldi's march.

November 14th, Peer Gynt published.

1868   *February.* Resumes work on Julian drama.

June. Berchtesgaden. Begins to write *The League of Youth* (*De unges forbund*).

October. Moves to Dresden.

1869 *Winter.* Writing *The League of Youth* (*De unges forbund*).

Spring. The League of Youth (*De unges forbund*) finished.

Summer. Mother dies.

July 3rd, financial grant from Norwegian Government for studies in Sweden.

July. Stockholm. Delegate to Nordic orthographic conference.

Receives Vasa Order from King Carl XV.

Appointed as delegate at opening of Suez Canal.

September. The League of Youth (*De unges forbund*) published.

October. Leaves for opening of Suez Canal.

November. Passes through Suez Canal on one of the first boats. Returns to Dresden via Paris. Acquires a Turkish decoration.

1870 *Spring.* Revises *The Pretenders* (*Kongs-emnerne*).

July. Franço-Prussian War.

Visits Denmark and returns to Dresden.

Plans for text of an opera on Sigurd Jorsalfar.

October. Sends his first short autobiography to Peter Hansen.

December. Revises poems of past twenty years.

Earliest traces of plans for *Pillars of Society.*

1871 *Winter.* Revises poems.

Correspondence with Georg Brandes.

Finishes and rewrites part one of his Julian drama, *Emperor and Galilean* (*Kejser og Galilæer*).

1872 *Spring.* Reads Brandes's *Main Currents in Nineteenth Century Literature.*

Summer spent in Bohemia and Austria. Five to six weeks in Berchtesgaden.

Winter. Occupied with part two of *Emperor and Galilean* (*Kejser og Galilæer*).

1873 *October 16th, Emperor and Galilean* (*Kejser og Galilæer*) published.

Appointed judge at international art exhibition in Vienna.

Created Knight of St. Olaf by King Oscar II.

Begins to be known in Germany and England.

1874 *Summer.* Returns to Norway. Spends $2\frac{1}{2}$ months in Oslo. One week in Stockholm at international congress of archaeologists. Begins to be known in France.

September 10th, torchlight procession of Norwegian students in his honour. Considered as a conservative. Reaction against conservatism begins.

1875 *Spring.* Moves to Munich. Gives up verse for prose.

1876   *June.* Guest of Duke of Saxe-Meiningen at performance of *The Pretenders* (*Kongs-emnerne*). Decorated with the Ernestine Order.

      Summer spent at Gossensass.

1877   Father dies.

      July. Pillars of Society (*Samfundets støtter*) ready for press.

      October 11th, Pillars of Society (*Samfundets støtter*) published.

1878   *Summer.* Gossensass.

      September. Rome.

      October. First notes for *A Doll's House* (*Et dukkehjem*) written.

1879   *January.* Makes proposals for women's votes and a lady librarian in the Scandinavian Club.

      February 27th, speech in favour of above motions. Anger at their rejection.

      September. A Doll's House (*Et dukkehjem*) finished. Moves to Munich.

      December 4th, A Doll's House (*Et dukkehjem*) published.

1880   *Summer.* Berchtesgaden with Jonas Lie. Bad weather.

      Autumn. Munich. Anger at ecclesiastical narrow-mindedness in Norway.

      Late Autumn. Rome.

1881   *Winter.* Rome. First notes for *Ghosts* (*Gengangere*) written.

      December. Ghosts (*Gengangere*) published.

      Begins immediately to write *The Enemy of the People* (*En folkefiende*).

1882   *Spring.* Writing *The Enemy of the People* (*En folkefiende*).

      November 28th, The Enemy of the People (*En folkefiende*) published.

1883   *February.* Earliest plans for *The Wild Duck* (*Vildanden*).

      Revises *The Feast at Solhaug* (*Gildet på Solhaug*).

1884   *February.* Impeachment of Norwegian ministers.

      June 30th, leaves Rome for Gossensass.

      September. The Wild Duck (*Vildanden*) finished.

      November 11th, The Wild Duck (*Vildanden*) published.

1885   *Spring.* Intends to move to Norway.

      June. Visits Christiania.

      June 10th, attended debate on Kielland in Norwegian Parliament.

      June 14th, speech to workers in Trondheim.

      Stays at Molde. Meets Dietrichson and Snoilsky.

      Passes through Bergen and meets Rikke Holst (now Mrs. Tresselt) again.

      September. Christiania. Refuses torchlight procession arranged by conservative students.

September 30*th*, leaves for Copenhagen. Hailed by Brandes and Danish students as a radical.

October. Settles in Munich.

November. Elected honorary member of Norwegian radical students' society. First notes for *Rosmersholm.*

1886 *Spring.* Georg Brandes falls out with radical Norwegian students. Ibsen becomes sceptical of radicals. Occupied with *Rosmersholm.*

June. First draft of play with title *White Horses* finished.

September 27*th*, play remodelled and finished as *Rosmersholm.*

November 23*rd, Rosmersholm* published.

December 22*nd*, guest of Duke of Saxe-Meiningen at a performance of *Ghosts* (*Gengangere*) and elevated to rank of Commander of Ernestine Order, first class.

1887 *July.* Visits Danish coastal town of Sæby. Meets Danish actress Engelcke Friis. Rejuvenation.

September 12*th*, Gothenburg. Happy mood. Political interests waning.

September 24*th*, Stockholm. Speech referring to his optimism.

October 1*st*, annoys Brandes by consenting to be the guest of the unpolitical students union.

Returns to Munich. Death of his publisher and friend, F. Hegel.

1888 *June.* Begins to write *The Lady from the Sea* (*Fruen fra havet*).

September 30*th*, play finished.

November 28*th, The Lady from the Sea* (*Fruen fra havet*) published.

1889 *Summer* spent in Gossensass. Affection for German painter Helene Raff and Viennese girl Emilie Bardach.

November. First notes on *Hedda Gabler.*

1890 *October* 7*th*, finishes first draft of *Hedda Gabler* in Munich.

November. Play revised.

December 16*th, Hedda Gabler* published.

1891 *July.* Leaves Munich to settle in Norway.

July 16*th*, arrives in Christiania. Tours to the North Cape.

August 7*th*, returns to Christiania. Welcomed by all parties.

October. Attends Knut Hamsun's lectures on the decadence of modern literature.

Settles permanently in Christiania.

1892 *July.* Work on *The Master Builder* (*Bygmester Solness*).

August 9*th-September* 19*th*. First draft of play.

October. Final version finished.

December 12*th, The Master Builder* (*Bygmester Solness*) published.

1894   *July.* Draft of *Little Eyolf* (*Lille Eyolf*).
      October. Final version completed.
      November. Play printed.
      December 11*th, Little Eyolf* (*Lille Eyolf*) published.

1895   Moves from Victoria Terasse to Arbins Gate.

1896   *April.* Work on *John Gabriel Borkman.*
      August 26*th,* first draft finished.
      October 18*th,* final version completed.
      December 15*th, John Gabriel Borkman* published.

1897   *June.* Plans for new play.

1898   *March* 20*th,* seventieth birthday. Dinner in Christiania. Travels from Christiania to Copenhagen. Festivities in his honour. Gala performance of *Brand.* Decorated by King Christian IX with Grand Cross of the Dannebrog Order. Travels to Sweden. Honoured in Stockholm. Oscar II decorates him with the Grand Cross of the Order of the Northern Star. Collected editions of Ibsen's works published by Fischer in Germany and Gyldendal in Denmark.
      August. Work on *When We Dead Awaken* (*Når vi døde vågner*).

1899   *February* 20*th,* first dated notes for play.
      September. Attends opening of the National Theatre in Christiania.
      November 22*nd,* final version completed.
      December 19*th, When We Dead Awaken* (*Når vi døde vågner*) published.

1900   *Winter.* Contemplates a fresh work.
      Spring. First stroke. Right side partially paralysed.
      Summer spent at Sandefjord undergoing a cure for erysipelas. Sides with British imperialism against Norwegian opinion in the Boer War.

1901   Further mention of projected new work.
      Second stroke. Unable to walk or write. Increasing mental and physical debility.

1902-1906   Bedridden.

1906   *May* 23*rd,* 2.30 p.m., dies.

SELECT BIBLIOGRAPHY

EDITIONS OF IBSEN'S WORKS

Hundreårsutgave. Samlede verker. Oslo. Gyldendal. Begun 1929. 20 vols. (not completed).

Samlede digterverker. Standardutgave ved Didrik Aarup Seip. Kristiania, København. Gyldendal. 1918.

Samlede vaerker. Kristiania. København. 1914. Jubilaeumsutgaven.

Samlede vaerker. Kristiania. København. Gyldendal. 1906-1907. Mindeutgaven.

Samlede vaerker. København. 1898-1902. Folkeutgaven.

Breve. Udgivne med indledning og oplysninger af Halvdan Koht og Julius Elias. København. Gyldendal. 1904.

Efterladte Skrifter. Udgivne af Halvdan Koht og Julius Elias. Kristiania. Gyldendal. 1909.

Tyve brev fra Henrik Ibsen. Utgitt i faksimile med innledning og oplysninger av Wilhelm Munthe. Oslo. 1932.

Collected Works. Entirely revised and edited by William Archer. London. W. Heinemann. 1908-1910. 11 vols.

Collections of manuscripts of plays, poems and letters in Oslo University Library, Bergens Museum and Bergens Teatermuseum.

BIBLIOGRAPHICAL WORKS

FIRKINS, INA FEN EYCK. *Henrik Ibsen.* A bibliography of criticism and biography. New York. 1921.

HALVORSEN, J. B. *Norsk Forfatterlexikon III.*

PETTERSEN, HJALMAR. *Henrik Ibsen.* Bedømt af samtid og eftertid. Et forsøg ved Hjalmar Pettersen. Oslo. 1928.

PETTERSEN, HJALMAR. *Bibliotheca Norvegica.* Vols. II, IV and V.

BIOGRAPHY AND CRITICISM

ARCHER, WILLIAM. *Translations of plays, articles and introductions to collected works.*

BAB, JULIUS. *Der Mensch auf der Bühne. Eine Dramaturgie für Schauspieler. Achtes Heft: Durch das Drama der Franzosen und Ibsens.* Berlin. 1923.

BERGGRAV, EIVIND OG BULL, FRANCIS. *Ibsens sjelelige krise.* Oslo. Gyldendal. 1937.

BERGSØE, VILHELM. *Henrik Ibsen paa Ischia og 'Fra Piazza del Popolo'. Erindringer fra Aarene* 1863-1869. København, 1907.

APPENDIX

BLANC, T. *Henrik Ibsen og Christiania Theater* 1850-1899. Kristiania, 1906.

BOYESEN, H. H. *A commentary on the works of Henrik Ibsen.* London. 1894.

BRANDES, GEORG. *Aesthetiske Studier.* København. 1868, 1888.
Det moderne Gjennembruds Maend. København. 1883, 1891.
Henrik Ibsen. København. 1898.

BULL, FRANCIS. *Studier og streiftog.* Oslo. 1931.

BØDTKER, SIGURD. *Kristiania-premierer gjennem 30 aar. Sigurd Bødtkers teaterartikler.* Vols. I-II. Kristiania. 1923-1924.

CAMPBELL, T. M. *Hebbel, Ibsen and the analytical exposition.* Heidelberg. 1922.

COUSSANGE, JACQUES DE. *L'influence française dans l'œuvre d'Ibsen.* (*Revue de littérature comparée*, 1925, pp. 298-305.)

DIETRICHSON, LORENTZ. *Svundne Tider*, I, IV. Kristiania. 1896, 1917.

DOUMIC, RENÉ. *De Scribe à Ibsen. Causeries sur le théâtre contemporain.* Paris. 1901.

DUE, CHRISTOPHER. *Erindringer fra Henrik Ibsens Ungdomsaar.* København. 1909.

EHRHARD, AUGUSTE. *Henrik Ibsen et le théâtre contemporain.* Paris. 1892.

EITREM, H. *Ibsen og Grimstad.* Oslo. 1940.

GOSSE, EDMUND W. *Articles, translations and introductions to works. Studies in the Literature of Northern Europe.* London. 1879, 1883.
Northern Studies. London. 1890.
Ibsen. London. 1907.

GRAN, GERHARD. *Henrik Ibsen. Liv og verker.* 2 vols. Kristiania. 1918.

GUTHRIE, THOMAS ANSTEY. *Mr. Punch's pocket Ibsen.* London. 1893, 1895.

HALVORSEN, JENS BRAAGE. *Bibliografiske Oplysniger til Henrik Ibsens Samlede Vaerker.* København. 1901.

HEIBERG, GUNNAR. *Ibsen og Bjornson paa scenen.* Kristiania. 1918. (Also articles and speeches and *Salt og sukker*, 1924.)

HØST, SIGURD. *Henrik Ibsen.* Paris. Stock. 1924.
Ibsens diktning og Ibsen selv. Oslo. Gyldendal. 1927.

JAEGER, HENRIK. *Henrik Ibsen 1826-1888.* Oslo. Translations in English and German, biographical articles and criticism.

KEHLER, HENNING. *Studier i det Ibsenske Drama.* Edda IV, 1915. V, 1916.

KIHLMAN, ERIK. *Ur Ibsen-dramatikens idéhistoria.* En studie i dansk-norsk litteratur. Helsingfors. 1921.

SELECT BIBLIOGRAPHY

KOHT, HALVDAN. *Henrik Ibsen. Eit diktarliv.* 2 vols. Aschehoug, Oslo. 1928-1929.

LINDER, STEN. *Ibsen, Strindberg och andra.* Stockholm. 1936.

LORD, FRANCES. *Life of Henrik Ibsen.* London. 1882. (Also translations.)

LUGNÉ-POE. *Ibsen.* 1936. Paris.

NISSEN, INGJALD. *Sjelelige kriser i menneskets liv. Henrik Ibsen og den moderne psykologi.* Oslo. 1931.

PAULSEN, JOHN. *Erindringer.* København. 1903.
Samliv med Ibsen. København og Kristiania. 1906, 1913. (Other reminiscences and articles.)

PROZOR, MORITZ (French translator). *Translations and introductions.*

REICH, EMIL. *Aus Leben und Dichtung.* Leipzig. 1911.
Henrik Ibsens Dramen (Dresden, Leipzig). 1894, 1900, 1903, 1906, 1909, 1918, 1925.

SARCEY, FRANCISQUE. *Quarante ans de théâtre.* Paris. 1902.

SHAW, GEORGE BERNARD. *The quintessence of Ibsenism.* London. 1891, 1913.

WAIS, KURT, K. I. *Henrik Ibsen und das Problem des Vergangenen.* Stuttgart. 1931.

WEIGAND, HERMAN J. *The modern Ibsen. A reconsideration.* New York. 1925.

WICKSTEED, PHILIP H. *Four lectures on Henrik Ibsen dealing chiefly with his metrical works.* London. 1892.

WIESENER, A. M. *Henrik Ibsen og det norske Theater i Bergen 1851-1857.* Bergen. 1928.
Katalog over Bergens Museums manuskriptsamling.

WOERNER, ROMAN. *Henrik Ibsen.* 2 vols. Munich. 1900, 1910, 1912, 1923.

ZUCKER, A. E. *Ibsen, the master builder.* London. 1930.